Robyn Wi[illegible] [illegible]ed guide to eat[illegible] [illegible]mer journalist turned r[illegible] [illegible] owns the Bleeding Heart Restau[illegible] and Brasserie in London's historic Bleeding Heart Yard off Hatton Garden. Despite the Englishness of its location (it features in Dickens' *Little Dorrit*) the Bleeding Heart has a French brigade both in the kitchen and front of house. When not at the Bleeding Heart, Mrs Wilson spends much of her time in France where she has a house in the northern Provence village of Gigondas.

The Travellers' French Food and Wine Dictionary

ROBYN WILSON

To Willy,
who knows that a meal without wine
is like a day without sunshine.

A *Warner* Book

First published in Great Britain by
Sphere Books Ltd 1990
Reprinted by Warner Books 1994

Typeset by Leaper & Gard Ltd., Bristol, England
Printed in England by Clays Ltd, St Ives plc

ISBN 0 7515 1242 7

Warner Books
A Division of
Little, Brown and Company (UK) Ltd
Brettenham House
Lancaster Place
London WC2E 7EN

Contents

Introduction 1

Restaurant Phrases . . . 6

Glossary 11

THE FRENCH FOOD AND WINE DICTIONARY

French – English 13

English – French 185

Recommended Reading and Bibliography 248

Acknowledgments

Dominique Cure, Le Chef, Bleeding Heart

Christophe Jerome, Sous-Chef, Bleeding Heart

Jean-Claude Serentha, Maitre d'Hotel, Bleeding Heart

Emanuel Hardonnier, Sommelier, Bleeding Heart

and a special thanks to Nicholas Rutland, who created a unique computer programme for *The French Food and Wine Dictionary*.

Introduction

The French Food and Wine Dictionary is designed to help travellers to France — whether they are committed Francophiles or first-time visitors — take a more adventurous approach to French food and wine. Whether sampling the menu dégustation in a chic Parisian restaurant, tossing-up between the plats-du-jour in a provincial brasserie, or shopping for a picnic in a tiny country town, you can use the Food and Wine Dictionary to help you order the foods you've always fancied but never knew how to ask for. Help is now at hand.

One of the joys of eating in France is the diversity of its regional foods. Travel from Normandy into neighbouring Brittany and the whole menu changes: not just the main courses, but the cheeses and desserts, even the digestifs are distinctly different.

This can create a slight problem for the travelling diner. A word or phrase that means one thing in Northern France can mean something quite different in Provence. Some food terms have three or four different meanings depending which region of France you are eating in. The description 'á la Richelieu', for instance, which literally translates as 'in the style of Cardinal Richelieu' can mean a) coated in egg and breadcrumbs and fried with herb butter; b) garnished with stuffed tomatoes, mushrooms, braised lettuce and potatoes; c) a large iced cake; d) a pear poached in red wine and served with redcurrant jelly and cream.

Equally confusingly, the spelling of even a quite simple word can change every time you cross a regional frontier. The word for a maize-flour batter cake usually topped with cherries is known variously as: mias, millas, millat, millia, milliard, milliat and millot.

The best answer is, if in doubt, order it anyway: you are more likely to be pleasantly surprised than disappointed. And if you really don't like it, the section headed Restaurant Phrases, on page 6 will tell you how to change it.

But first, here are a few simple suggestions that may increase the pleasure you can get from eating out in France.

Reservations

Even if you suspect that your chosen restaurant will be less than a quarter full, it's worth making a reservation. If only because it cheers the chef to know he has at least two covers tonight, and the maitre d' gets to know your name (useful if you plan to visit the restaurant more than once). You are also more likely to get a better table if you book, than if you turn up on spec.

If you have made a booking some days, or weeks, previously at a particular restaurant it is worth confirming your booking on the day. It is entirely possible that the receptionist was being chatted up by one of the waiters when you phoned two weeks ago and put you in for the wrong day. If you particularly want a table by the window, or on the terrace, make this clear at the time you make your booking.

If, on arrival, you don't like the table they have given you, ask for another. But don't expect them to put you on a table for four, when there are only two of you. Being seated on what you consider to be the least desirable table in the room is the worst way to start an evening out.

The Menu

Usually the menu du jour/menu conseillé is much better value than eating à la carte, off the main menu. But popular restaurants often restrict the times (even days) that they serve their cheap menus. It is only when you have decided that the 75 franc menu has all your favourite dishes on it, that you can see in the small print at the bottom that it is only served at lunchtimes or on weekdays only. (See Restaurant Phrases for details.)

The Wine

Given that the French are geographically somewhat chauvinistic when it comes to wine (it is hard to get a decent Loire red when you are eating in Burgundy), it is best to drink locally. If you don't know the local wines, ask your waiter. He may not know much about vintages, but he will certainly know which local wines are popular amongst his customers.

If the wine list is light on white wines, and this is especially true of smaller restaurants in the Rhône and Provence, try a rosé or even a red wine, well chilled, with the fish. A light fruity chilled red will do much more for your red mullet than a dull indifferent white.

If you think your wine is off (and this can happen even in the best of restaurants), tell your waiter immediately, and ask him to change it for another. It is not as if the cost of the bottle comes out of his patron's profits for the evening: the wine will simply be sent back to the restaurant's supplier in return for a refund.

The Bill

Do check your bill. In a busy restaurant, it is entirely possible that the over-worked waiter, or the new cashier, has accidentally charged you for the bottle of wine that was consumed on the table next to you. Or charged you for a whole bottle instead of a half. Perhaps the cashier had trouble deciphering the waiter's handwriting, or maybe she hit the wrong button on the new computerised cash register. Over-charging in most restaurants is usually caused by human error; it is rarely malicious.

In France now all restaurant bills must, by law include 15 percent service charge. There is no need to leave anything extra. However if you have had exceptionally good service you may want to make a small gesture to your waiter, especially if you are planning to return in the very near future.

The Waiter

Despite a surprisingly widely-held belief that French waiters undergo special training in unhelpfulness, obstructiveness and general aggression this is generally quite untrue.

What is true is that they take themselves much more seriously than many of their Anglo-Saxon counterparts. Unlike many waiters and waitresses in the UK who are students or resting actors, filling in time until they can get what to them is a proper job, most French waiters are professionals: waiting is what they do for a living and they have no plans to rush off and do something else. They take themselves and their jobs seriously, and they expect their customers to do so as well.

If you need to catch your waiters attention, call him Monsieur (NEVER garçon, and never ever snap your fingers at a French waiter or you will wait all evening to be served). And always finish each request, however simple with the obligatory 's'il vous plaît'.

The French are on the whole a much more formal race than the Anglo-Saxons, and would never even buy a baguette from the corner boulangerie without first greeting Madame behind the counter with a 'bonjour, madame', followed by a liberal sprinkling of 's'il vous plait, madame' and a final 'merci, madame' and 'au revoir, madame'.

Generally speaking the more courteous you are to your waiter — indicating that you too believe that eating out is a pleasure to be taken seriously — the better your service will be, and the more you will enjoy your meal.

Restaurant Phrases

Booking

I would like to book a table for lunch today/dinner tonight
Bonjour, je voudrais réserver une table pour déjeuner aujourd'hui/dîner ce soir, s'il vous plaît

For two/four/six people
Pour deux/quatre/six personnes

At noon/1.30pm/7.45pm (or 19.45)
A midi/une heure trente/huit heures moins le quart (or dix-neuf quarante cinq)

Do we need to book for lunch/dinner?
Faut-il réserver pour déjeuner/diner?

I would like to confirm our booking for lunch
Je voudrais confirmer notre réservation pour déjeuner

In the name of Smith
Au nom de Smith

For two, at nine thirty (or 21.30)
Pour deux à neuf heures et demi (vingt et un, trente)

We would like a table on the terrace/by the window, please
Nous aimerions une table sur la terrasse/à la fenêtre, s'il vous plaît

At the Restaurant

Good evening, we have a reservation in the name of Smith. Two at 8.30pm

Bonsoir, nous avons une réservation au nom de Smith pour deux personnes a vingt heure trente

This table by the door is a little draughty. Could we change it?
Cette table à côté de la porte est au courant d'air. Serait-il possible de la changer, s'il vous plaît?

We would like to order some aperitifs, please
Nous voudrions commander des apértifs, s'il vous plaît.

With lemon and ice please
Avec du citron, et de la glace, s'il vous plaît.

No, thank you, we won't have aperitifs. Just the wine list, please
Merci, nous ne prendrons pas d'apéritif. Seulement la carte des vins, s'il vous plaît.

The Menus

The set price menu is served:
Le Menu Prix-Fixe/Le Menu Conseillé est servi,

only at lunch times
seul dejeuner:

only on weekdays
seul semaine

not on Sundays
sauf le dimanche

not at weekends
sauf les fins de semaine

not on public holidays
sauf les jours feries

any change to the set menu will incur an extra cost
tout changement au menu implique un supplément

Yes, we are ready to order. Two of the 75 franc menus, please

Oui, monsieur, nous sommes prêt pour commander. Deux menus à soixante-quinze francs, s'il vous plaît.

We are going to eat from the à la carte menu tonight.
Nous mangerons à la carte ce soir.

What does the chef recommend today?
Qu'est'ce que le chef recommande aujourd'hui?

Could you recommend any local specialities?
Pourriez-vous nous recommander les spécialités de la region, s'il vous plaît?

What is the dish/the fish of the day?
Qu'est-ce que c'est le plat/le poisson du jour?

Does the main course come with vegetables?
Le plat principal, est-il garni?

I will have a mixed salad with the main course
Je voudrais une salade panaché avec le plat principal.

Could you bring another knife/fork/spoon/plate?
Pourriez-vous apporter un(e) autre couteau/fourchette/cuillère/assiette?

This is not what I ordered
Ce n'est pas ce que j'ai commandé.

Could I change this dish for another, please?
Est-ce que je puis changer ce plat pour un autre, s'il vous plaît?

No cheese thank you. Just dessert.
Pas de fromage. Seulement un dessert.

Can you recommend a good local cheese?
Pourriez-vous nous recommander un bon fromage du coin?

This one here, is it cows' or goats' cheese?
Celui-ci, c'est du chèvre ou de la vache?

Some more bread please.
Encore du pain, s'il vous plaît.

Do you have any brown bread?
Est-ce que vous avez du pain complet?

The Wine

Which local wine do you recommend to go with the starters?
Qu'est que vous recommandez comme vin du region pour aller avec les hors d'oeuvres?

And for the main course?
Et pour les plats principaux?

Do you have the rosé in half bottles?
Est-ce que vous avez le rosé, en demi?

I would like a red/white that is fruity/full-bodied/dry/well-chilled
Je voudrais un vin rouge/vin blanc/fruité/corsé/sec/bien frais.

And a glass/bottle of fizzy/still mineral water
Et un verre/une bouteille de l'eau minérale gazeuse/non-gazeuse.

This white wine is not chilled enough
Ce vin blanc n'est pas assez frais.

Could you bring us an ice-bucket please?
Pourriez-vous nous apporter un seau à glace, s'il vous plaît?

Could you please open the red wine now?
Voudriez-vous déboucher le vin rouge maintenant, s'il vous plaît?

Could we have another bottle?
Une autre bouteille, s'il vous plaît?

The wine is maderised/corked. Could you bring us another bottle?
Le vin est maderisé/bouchonné. Pourriez-vous nous apporter une autre bouteille?

We would like two glasses of champagne with the dessert
Nous voudrions deux coupes de champagne avec les desserts, s'il vous plaît.

Do you do a dessert wine by the glass?
Auriez-vous un vin doux au verre?

Do you have any cigars?
Avez-vous des cigares?

Could we have an ashtray, please?
Un cendrier, s'il vous plaît?

Where are the toilets?
Où sont les toilettes, s'il vous plaît?

Could we have the bill please?
L'addition, s'il vous plaît?

We are in a bit of a hurry.
Nous sommes un peu pris par le temps.

Do you take credit cards/eurocheques?
Est-ce que vous acceptez les cartes de credit/les eurocheques?

The service charge is included, isn't it?
Le service est compris, non?

Could we speak to the head waiter/manager/proprietor?
Serait-il possible de parler au maître d'hotel/gérant/patron?

Could you order us a taxi please. We're going to . . .?
Pourriez-vous appeler un taxi, s'il vous plaît. Nous allons à . . .?

Thank you, we enjoyed the meal very much. Goodbye.
Merci. C'etait tres bien. À bientôt.

Glossary

French to English:

'à la' — where word is followed by 'à la', this indicates the style of presentation or garnish e.g. bourgeoise, 'à la' means the dish is usually served with carrot, onion and bacon. However because of tremendous variations in French cooking from region to region the presentation of a dish may differ from that stated.

Wines: after each wine listed the letters *ac/aoc/vdqs/vdp/vdt/vdn* will appear. These letters denote the classification of the wine and mean as follows:
ac/aoc: appellation d'origine controlee. This is the highest of the wine classifications and indicates that the wine meets specific requirements in relation to the area it comes from, the grapes it is made from, and the degree of alcohol it contains.
vdqs: vin delimité de qualite supérieur. This classification is below *ac*, but also indicates that the wine comes from a specifically controlled area of production.
vdp: vin de pays. The third classification of French wine, denoting that the wine comes from a particular area but it is not quite as good as vdqs.
vdt: vin de table. Ordinary table wine with no classification.
vdn: vin doux naturel. Strong sweet wine, fortified with brandy.

English to French:

All French nouns are followed by m or f to indicate whether they are masculine (le) or feminine (la). A French noun beginning with a consonant will always be preceded by 'l'' regardless of its gender.

Where there is more one than French word for its English counterpart, the first-named word will generally be the one in more common usage. Though with so many regional variations, this is unfortunately not always the case.

Abadèche	Type of sea bass
Abaisse	Layer of sponge cake
Abat-faim	'Hunger-beater' — a fairly hefty dish at start of meal
Abatis de volaille	Chicken giblets
Abats	Offal
Abats de volaille	Giblets
Abignades	Goose tripe on fried bread
Ablette	Tiny freshwater fish
Abondance	Watered-down wine
Abondance	Small firm round cows' cheese
Abricot	Apricot
Abricoter	To glaze with jam or jelly
Abricotine	Apricot liqueur
Absinthe	Powerful liqueur made from distilled wormwood leaves
Abusseau	Small sea smelt
AC	Controlled appellation: system of classifying wine
Acanthe	Salad leaf in Southern France
Acarne	Type of seabream
Acave	Type of snail
Aceline	Freshwater fish
Acerbe	Astringent, tart
Acescent	Wine is slightly sour

Acetomel	Sweet-sour preserve for fruit
Achard	Fruit or vegetable pickle
Ache	Wild celery
Acidité	Acidity, sourness, tartness
Acidulée	Acidulated
Acquette	Aromatic liqueur with cinammon, cloves and nutmeg
Actinie	Sea anemone
Addition	Bill
Adobo	Provence stew of artichokes, tomatoes and wine
Adour	With a ham and sorrel stuffing
Aeglé	Ugli fruit, similar to grapefruit
Affiné	Refined
Africaine, à l'	With aubergines, tomatoes
Agathoise	Agde-style: usually cuttlefish, stuffed, then boiled
Âge	Age, especially of spirits
Agenais	Agen-style: usually with goose or goose fat
Agneau	Lamb
Agneau de lait	Milk-fed lamb
Agneau de pré-salé	Lamb from the salt marshes
Agnelet	Baby lamb
Agnelle	Ewe lamb
Agnès sorel	Garnish, usually with mushrooms and ox tongue
Agon	Type of sardine
Agoursi	Salted cucumbers
Agras	Almond and grape juice iced drink
Aigle-de-mer	Breton term for skate

Aiglefin	Haddock
Aigo-boulido	Provençale garlic broth
Aigo-sau	Garlicky fish soup or stew
Aigo-sau d'iou	Leek, garlic, onion soup with poached eggs
Aigre	Sour
Aigre de cèdre	Fruit of South French citron, used in type of lemonade
Aigre-doux	Sweet and sour
Aigrelette, sauce	Sharp sauce of tart grape juice
Aigrette	Savoury fritter
Aigrossade	Provençale dish of garlic, chickpeas, beans and potatoes
Aiguillat	Spiny shark, dogfish
Aiguillat tacheté	Spur dog shark
Aiguille	Name for garfish
Aiguillette	Narrow piece of meat, poultry or game usually sliced from breast
Ail	Garlic
Ail vert	Very young garlic
Aile	Wing
Ailicuit	Stewed poultry wings, giblets
Aïllade	Sauce of garlic, herbs and tomatoes
Aillé	Garlic-flavoured, garlicky
Aillee	Green part of garlic clove
Aillerons	Chicken wingtips
Aïoli	Garlic sauce
Air, pommes en l'	Fried slices of apple
Airelle	Cranberry
Aisy	Soured whey

Aisy-cendré	Strong, ash-coated cows' cheese cured in marc
Alambic	Traditional aparatus for distilling spirits
Albarelle	Edible fungus from chestnuts
Alberge	Type of peach
Albert, sauce	Type of horseradish sauce
Albigeoise	Albi style: usually with tomato, ham and potatoes
Albuféra, sauce	Sweet pepper sauce
Alcool	Alcohol
Alcool-blanc	Clear alcohol, eau de vie
Alénois	With watercress
Alésienne, tripes à l'	Tripe with carrots, tomatoes and celery
Alevin	Young fish or fry
Algérienne, à l'	Usually cooked with oil and tomatoes
Algue	Edible sea bird
Algues	Seaweed
Alicot	Stewed poultry wings, giblets
Aligot	Fresh cow cheese from Auvergne
Aligot	Purée of potato, garlic, cheese
Aligoté	Burgundy's principal white wine grape
Alimentation	Food
Alise	Type of rowanberry, used in Alsace for liqueur
Alisson	Name for sea urchin
Alkermès	Red cordial with nutmeg, cinnamon and cloves
All-grenat	Sauce for snails: usually garlic and peppers

Allache	Type of sardine
Alleluia	Small cake
Allemande, sauce	German-style thick egg sauce
Allemande, à l'	German-style: a sour cream sauce for game; with mash potatoes
Allière	Garlic-flavoured salad leaf
Allongé'	Diluted or extended
Allumettes	Small, oven-baked pastry strips
Allumettes	Matches
Allumettes, pommes	Very thin potato chips
Alma, poire	Pear poached in red wine
Alose	Shad fish
Alose finte	Type of shad fish
Alouette	Skylark
Alouette de mer	Sandpiper, type of snipe
Alouette sans tête	Stuffed rolls of veal
Aloxe-Corton AC	Very good red, white burgundy from Côte de Beaune
Aloyau	Sirloin of beef
Alphée	Type of large prawn
Alphonse-la-Vallée	Black table grape
Alsacienne, à l'	Alsace style: usually with sauerkraut, ham, sausage
Amaigri	Thin, especially of wine
Amande	Almond
Amande vert	Soft unripe very sour almond
Amande-de-mer	Small shellfish
Ambassadeur	Usually garnished with truffles
Ambigu	Small cold buffet meal
Amboise, tourraine AC	White, rosé, some reds from Loire

Ambonnay	Champagne village producing red Bouzy rouge wines
Ambrette	Type of pear
Ambrosie	Herb tea from Ambrosier plant
Ameleon	Type of cider
Amenlon	Almond pastry
Amer picon	Orange and gentian aperitif
Amer, amère	Bitter
Americaine, amoricaine, à l'	Brandy, wine and tomato sauce
Amiral, à l'	With mushrooms, fried mussels, truffles and crayfish tails
Ammocète	Lamprey-type fish
Amou	Tangy sheep's cheese
Amourettes	Bone marrow
Amplovo	Another name for anchovy
Amuse-gueule	Appetiser
Amusette	Appetiser
Amygdalin	Of almonds
Anacarde	Cashew
Ananas	Pineapple
Anchoïade	Anchovy and garlic paste
Anchois	Anchovy
Anchois de norvège	Type of sprat
Ancienne, à l'	Traditional
Andalouse	Tomato and green pepper sauce
Andouille	Pork-tripe sausage, served cold
Andouillette	Sausage of pigs intestine stuffed with tripe, served hot

Âne	Donkey: meat used for pate, sausages
Anémone de mer	Sea anemone
Ânesse	Ass
Aneth	Dill
Aneth doux	A name for fennel
Ange	Angel
Ange de mer	Angel shark, also monkfish
Angélique	Angelica
Anges à cheval	Angels on horseback (oysters wrapped in bacon)
Angevine	Table grape
Angevine, à la	Anjou-style, usually cooked in Anjou wine
Anglaise, à l'	English-style, fried with breadcrumbs (fish)
Anglaise, à l'	English-style, plain-boiled (meat)
Anglaise, crême	Egg-custard
Anglois	Type of plum tart
Anguille	Eel
Anguille de mer	Conger eel
Anguillettes	Small eels
Animelles	Lambs testicles, often called white kidneys
Anis vert	Sweet cumin
Anis	Aniseed
Anisette	Aniseed liqueur
Anjou, AC	Loire rosé, white and some red wines
Anna	Potato dish with cream, butter
Annot	Sheep's cheese
Anon	Breton name for haddock
Anone	Custard apple

Antiboise	Antibes-style: usually with garlic, tomatoes and sardines
Antillaise	Antilly islands style: usually with rum
Anversoise	Garnished with hop shoots
AOC	Appellation d'origine controlée: highest wine classification
Apéritif	Drink before meal
Aphie	Rockling
Apogon	Another term for red mullet
Appétit	Another name for chives
Aprémont, vin de Savoie, AC	Light white wine from Savoy
Apré	Harsh, rough (especially wine)
Apron	Small perch-like fish
Aqueux	Watery
Arachide	Peanut
Araignée, de mer	Type of crab
Arapède	Shellfish, similar to cockle
Arbenne	Mountain partridge
Arbin, vin de savoie AC	Red wine from Savoy
Arbois, AC	Light 'yellow' wine from Jura
Arbolade	Dessert of pear-flavoured custard
Arbouse	Cane apple berry, also digestif
Arc-en-ciel	Rainbow
Arcanette	A type of duck
Arcarchonnaises	Oysters from Arcachon near Bordeaux
Arche de noé	Type of clam
Archiduc, à l'	Usually with cream and paprika

Ardennaise	Usually with juniper berries
Ardoise	Traditional slang for bill
Arête	Fish-bone
Argenteuil	Usually with asparagus
Argentine	Silver fish
Ariègoise, à l'	Usually with cabbage, salt pork and kidney beans
Arlequine, à l'	Multi-coloured
Arlésienne	With tomato, aubergine and rice
Armagnac	Single-distilled brandy
Armillaire	Type of mushroom
Armoricaine	Type of oyster
Armotte	Cooked maize or polenta
Aromates	Herb or spice seasonings
Aromatisée	Flavoured with particular aroma
Arome	Smell
Aromes	Strong ewes' or goats' cheese
Arquebuse	Traditional aromatic herbal liqueur
Arrière-goût	After-taste
Arrigny	Cow cheese from Champagne
Arroche	Spinach-style vegetable
Arroser	To baste or moisten
Artésienne, à la	Usually cooked with beer
Artichaut	Artichoke
Artisanale	Peasant-style
Arvèze	Gentian-flavoured aperitif
Asco	Strong square goat cheese
Asperge	Asparagus
Aspergille	Small snail
Aspic	Cold dish covered with aspic

Assaisonné	Seasoned
Assaisonnement	Condiments, seasoning
Assiette	Plate
Assiette Anglaise	Plate of assorted cold meat
Assiette assortie	Assorted hors d'oeuvres
Astroderme	Brightly coloured fish, especially used in bouillabaisse
Athérine	Small smelt
Attendri	Tenderised
Attereau	Skewer for cooking
Attignole	Meatball
Au lieu de	Instead of
Aubance	White wine slopes in Loire
Aubazine	Herbal liqueur
Aubépine	Hawthorn
Auberge	Inn
Aubergine	Aubergine or egg-plant
Aubuis	Type of chalky soil in Touraine
Auguebelle	Herbal liqueur
Aujourd'hui	Today
Aulx	Garlic plural
Aumonière	Rolled-up pancake in shape of money bag
Aurin	Another name for grey mullet
Auriol	Another name for mackerel
Auriquette	Type of white bread
Aurore	Rich creamy cow cheese
Aurore, sauce	Creamy pink sauce with added tomato
Autrichienne, à l'	Austrian-style: usually with paprika, onions and cream
Autun	Soft nutty dry goat cheese

Auvergnat	Type of vine from Auvergne
Auvergnate, à l'	Usually with cabbage and salt pork
Auxerrois	White wine grape, especially in Alsace
Avec	With
Aveline	Hazelnut
Avenugle, dégustation à l'	Blind-tasting (as wine)
Avocat	Avocado
Avocette	Small wading bird, like a teal
Avoine	Oats
Axonge	Lard, of pork
Ay	Former capital of Champagne
Azi	Rennet
Azyme	Unleavened

Ba-ta-clan	Almond pastry dessert
Baba	Soft dough cake cooked in syrup, often rum soaked
Babeurre	Buttermilk
Bacile	Term for samphire
Bacon	Sliced packaged bacon
Badèche	Brown sea bass, also name for grouper
Badiane	Type of aniseed, also aniseed liqueur
Badoche	Provençale dried cod fish
Badoit	Brand of sparkling mineral water
Baeckoffa	Alsace stew of mutton, pork and beef in wine
Bagna cauda	Hot anchovy and oil dip
Baguette	Long white bread stick
Baguettes	Chopsticks
Baie	Berry
Baie de ronce	Term for blackberry
Baies roses	Term for pink peppercorns
Baigné	Bathed in
Bain-marie	Pot or dish for cooking over water
Bajaine	Small snail
Bajoue	Pig's cheek
Balaou	Saury or garfish, also needlefish

Baliste	Triggerfish
Ballon	Ball, ball-shape
Ballottines de volaille	Bundles of boned, stuffed poultry or meat
Balthazar	Large bottle, equivalent 16 bottles
Baltique	Small Baltic herring
Baluchons	Bundles (esp. of meat)
Balvet	Pea and vegetable soup
Bambelle	Freshwater fish, similar to carp
Bambou	Bamboo shoots
Banane	Banana
Banarut	Small snail
Bandol	Provence appellation, mainly white and rosé wines
Bandol, AC	Provençal red wine
Banille	Small flavourful pod, similar vanilla
Banon	Provençale soft ewes' cheese
Banon au poivre	Peppered soft round goat cheese
Banquière	Garnish of mushrooms and truffles
Banyuls, AC	Sweet red fortified wine from Roussillon region
Baptisé	Slang term for watered-down wine
Bar	Sea bass
Bar	Bar or café
Bar-comptoir	Bar counter, usually serving snacks
Baraquet	Type of haricot bean
Baraquille	Hot stuffed pastry
Barbadine	Passion fruit

Barbarée	Yellow rocket, similar cress
Barbarey	Soft round creamy cows' cheese
Barbarie	Barbary duck
Barbarin	Type of mullet
Barbarine	Vegetable marrow
Barbaroux	Provence grape variety
Barbe-à-papa	Candyfloss
Barbe-de-capucin	Wild chicory
Barbeau	Barbel fish, freshwater
Barbery	Small soft cows' cheese
Barbillon	Small barbel
Barboteur	Type of duck
Barbouillade	Stewed aubergine
Barbouille, poulet en	Chicken in sauce, thickened with blood
Barbue	Brill
Bardane	Burdock
Bardatte	Stuffed cabbage dish with hare and chestnuts
Barde	Slice of bacon or lard
Barge	Type of marsh bird
Bargencote	Small fig
Barigoule	Brown sauce with artichokes
Baril	Barrel: usually 72 litres
Barnache	Barnacle, limpet
Baron	Saddle and legs of carcass
Barquette	Little pastry boat
Barrique	Type of wine barrel: 225 litre capacity
Barsac, AC	Sweet white dessert wine from Bordeaux
Bartavelle	Type of partridge
Bas, basse	Low

Baselle	Type of spinach
Basilic	Basil
Basquaise, à la	Usually with tomatoes, peppers, rice; also ham, mushrooms or potato
Bastardeau	Bustard
Bâtard Montrachet, AC	Very good white burgundy from Cote de Beaune
Bâtarde	Name for long white bread loaf
Bâtarde, sauce	A thick butter and egg sauce
Batavia	Type of lettuce
Batelière	Pastry cases filled with seafood
Baton	Small thin loaf of bread
Bâtons	Small sticks of pastry
Battu	Beaten or whipped
Baudroie	Anglerfish or monkfish
Baudroise	Rockfish or dogfish
Baume	Balm, herb
Bavaroise	Creamy egg dessert served chilled
Bavaroise	Hot sweet milky drink usually with egg and liqueur
Bavette	Skirt of beef
Baveuse	Runny (as in omelette)
Baveuse	Blenny fish
Bayonne, jambon de	Cured ham
Béarn, AC	Light, dry whites, some reds and rosés from the Pyrennees
Béarnaise	Butter and egg yolk sauce, with shallots, wine, tarragon
Béatilles	Small pieces of poultry offal
Béatrice, salade	Salad of steamed green beans

Beaucaire	Salad of celery, ham and beetroot
Beauceronne, omelette	Omelette with bacon, potato and sorrel
Beaufort	Firm yellow cows' cheese
Beaujolais Blanc, AC	White wines grown in Beaujolais region of Burgundy
Beaujolais cru	Formerly nine now ten Beaujolais communes are classed as'cru' or special growth
Beaujolais Nouveau	Very young Beaujolais wine, usually shipped late November
Beaujolais Supérieur, AC	Beaujolais with higher alcohol content: more than ten per cent
Beaujolais, AC	Fruity reds from southern Burgundy
Beaujolais-Villages, AC	Better, older Beaujolais from forty listed Beaujolais villages
Beaulieu-sur-layon, AC	Sweet and dry whites from Loire
Beaumes de Venise	Very sweet whites and fruity reds from small Rhone village
Beaumont	Firm mild round cow cheese
Beaumont-sur-Vesle	Village in Champagne growing superior grapes
Beaune	Walled city in the heart of Burgundy
Beaune, AC	Good reds, some whites from Burgundy's wine capital
Beaupre de Roybon	Mild cow cheese from Savoie
Beauvilliers	Usually with spinach, tomato, brains and salsify

Bec	beak
Bec-plat	Spoonbill duck
Bec-pointu	A name for white skate
Bécard	Name for an old male salmon
Bécasse	Woodcock
Bécasse-de-mer	Another name for red mullet
Bécasseau	Young woodcock
Bécassine	Snipe
Bécau	Young snipe
Becfigue	Figpecker bird
Becfin	Small bird, also name for gourmet
Béchamel	White sauce of butter, flour, milk, onions and herbs
Bêche de mer	Sea cucumber, sea slug
Bedeu	A name for tripe
Beignet	Fritter
Belle de Juillet	Type of potato
Belle-angevine	Type of pear
Belle-chevreuse	Type of peach
Belle-et-bonne	Type of cooking pear
Belle-hélène	Usually with asparagus, truffles, mushrooms
Belle-hélène, poire	Poached pear, ice-cream, chocolate sauce
Bellegarde, clairette de, AC	Yellowy white wine from Languedoc-Roussillon
Bellet, AC	Red, rosé, white from small Provence appellation
Bellone	Type of fig
Belons	Flat oysters
Belugo	Type of sea bream
Belval	A mild firm cows' cheese
Benari	Small game bird, similar ortolan

Bénédict	Served with hollandaise sauce and ham
Bénédictine	Liqueur invented by Normandy monks
Bénédictine, morue	Salt cod pureed with mashed potato
Benoîte	A salad green
Berce	Cow parsnip
Bercy	Sauce of fish stock, wine and onions
Bergamotte	Type of citron or orange
Bergerac, AC	Red, white, rosé wines from South-Western France
Bergère, à la	Shepherdess-style
Berlingot	Type of peppermint candy
Bernache	Newly-harvested wine
Bernard l'ermite	Hermit-crab
Bernicle	Name for limpet
Bernique	Limpet
Berrichonne, à la	Usually cooked in the blood of the meat
Berton	Type of cheese fondue
Besaigre	Term for wine on the turn: almost sour
Besi	Dried, salted beef
Besi	Type of pear
Besugo	Basque dish of seabream, garlic and peppers
Bête	Beast
Bête rousse	Baby boar
Bethmale	Firm strong cows' cheese
Bétise	Tripe
Bette	Another name for chard
Betterave	Beetroot
Beuda	Type of clam

Beugnon	Ring-shaped fritter
Beurre	Butter
Beurre blanc	Sauce of butter, shallots and vinegar
Beurre noir	Browned butter with vinegar, capers and parsley
Beurré	Type of pear
Beurrier	Butter dish
Beursades	Pieces of baked pork
Bezuque	A name for sea bream
Biarotte	Biarritz-style: usually with mushrooms and potatoes
Biche	Doe
Bichique	Very tiny seafish
Bien cuit	Well done
Bière	Beer
Bière de gingembre	Ginger beer
Bière de menage	Homebrewed beer
Bière pression	Draught beer
Biftek	Beefsteak
Biftek à cheval	Steak with fried eggs on top
Biftek haché	Minced steak
Bigarade	Bitter orange
Bigarade, sauce	Sauce with oranges and curaçao
Bigarreau	Type of cherry
Bignon	Sweet fritter
Bignorneau	Winkle
Bigolot	Soft white rind cow cheese
Biguenée	Pancake with ham
Bijane	Cold soup of wine and bread
Billy by	Mussel soup
Biou	Another name for winkle
Bironne	Type of marrow

Bis	Wholemeal
Biscotin	Sweet biscuit
Biscotte	Rusk or type of crispbread
Biscuit	Biscuit
Biset	Type of wild pigeon
Bisque	Shellfish soup
Bissalé	Hot, buttered dough
Bistouille	Coffee with added spirits
Bitok	Meat patty in a sour cream sauce
Blagny, AC	Good red and white burgundies
Blanc, vin	White wine
Blanc de blancs	White wine from white grapes
Blanc de noirs	White wine from black grapes
Blanc fumé	Name for the Sauvignon grape
Blanc, blanche	White
Blanc-cassis	White wine and blackcurrant liqueur
Blanchailles	Whitebait
Blanche-neige	White meat in a white sauce
Blanchet	Clam
Blanchots	One of the seven premier Chablis vineyards
Blancs de volaille	Breast of spring chicken
Blanquette de Limoux, AC	Sparkling wine from Languedoc Roussillon region
Blanquette de volaille/veal	Stew of chicken/veal in blanket of white sauce
Blaye, Cote de, AC	Dry, medium and sweet whites from Bordeaux
Blé	Wheat

Blé noir	Term for buckwheat
Blé, Amidon de	Cornflour
Blet	Over-ripe
Blette	Chard
Bleu	Blue-veined as in cheese
Bleu	Very rare, as steak
Bleu d'auvergne	Blue-mould cows' cheese
Bleu de basillac	Blue sheep's cheese
Bleu de Bresse	Blue-mould cylindrical cows' cheese
Bleu de Causses	Large blue-mould cows' cheese
Bleu de Laqueuille	Strong soft blue cows' cheese
Bleu de Tignes	Cylindrical blue cows' cheese
Bleu du Quercy	Blue-mould cows' cheese
Bleu, au	See Truite
Blinis	Small buckwheat pancakes
Blond de veau	White veal stock
Blond de volaille	White chicken stock
Blond	Pale, also pale ale
Boeuf	Beef
Boeuf au gros sel	Beef, vegetable stew served with rock salt
Boeuf bouilli	Boiled beef
Boeuf haché	Minced beef
Boeuf Stroganoff	Beef with sour cream and mushrooms
Boeuf, à la mode	Beef cooked with vegetables
Bogaravelle	Type of sea bream
Bogue	Big-eyed bream
Bohémienne, à la	Usually with rice, tomatoes, peppers, onions and paprika
Bois	Wood, cooked over wood
Boisson	Drink or beverage

Boisson compris	Beverage included
Boîte	Tin or can
Boîte à thé	Tea-caddy
Boîtelle	Poached in white wine with mushrooms
Bol	Bowl
Bolée	Earthenware bowl for drinking cider
Bolet	Type of mushroom
Bombe	Frozen ice-cream mould
Bommes	Sweet whites from Sauternes commune in Bordeaux
Bon, bonne	Good
Bon appetit	Enjoy your meal
Bon-Chrétien	Cooking pear
Bon-henri	Wild spinach
Bonbon	Sweet
Bondard	Small soft smooth cows' cheese
Bondaroy au foin	Hay-coated soft round tangy cows' cheese
Bondon	Small soft smooth cows' cheese
Bonité	Bonito, a type of tuna
Bonité à ventre ray	Skipjack tuna
Bonitou	A name for mackerel
Bonne femme, à la	With white wine, shallot, mushroom and onion sauce
Bonne-bouche	Small snack or nibble
Bonnes Mares, AC	Good red burgundies from Cotes de Nuits
Bonnezeaux, AC	Sweet white wine from Anjou
Bonvalet	Almond cake with kirsch and ice-cream

Bordé de	Bordered with
Bordeaux supérieur, AC	Bordeaux reds with higher alcohol level
Bordeaux, AC	Region producing 'claret' reds, dry, medium and sweet white
Bordelaise	Sauce with wine, shallots, tomato and beef marrow
Bordure	Border
Borghèse	Usually with asparagus and chicken
Bosson macéré	Goats' cheese cured in oil, brandy and herbs
Bossu	Coffee with a shot of Calvados
Botrytis	The 'rot' on grapes needed to produce sweet wines
Bouc	Male goat
Bouchée	Small pastry case
Bouchère, à la	Butcher-style, usually served with beef
Boucherie	Butcher's shop
Bouches du Rhone, VDP	Reds or rosés from Provence
Bouchet	Name for cabernet franc grape
Bouchon	Cork
Boucot	Term for prawn
Boudin blanc	White pudding sausage with pork, bacon and onions
Boudin noir	Black pudding with pigs' blood, kidney fat and onions
Bouffi	Bloater
Bougie	Candle

Bougnette	Type of pork sausage
Bougon	A small, round goats' cheese
Bougras	Soup of sausage broth, cabbage, leek and potatoes
Bougros	Good white burgundy from Chablis appellation
Bouillabaisse	Fish soup or stew
Bouillabaisse borgne	Leek, onion, garlic soup with poached eggs
Bouillant	Boiling
Bouille d'avoin	Oatmeal porridge
Bouilleture	Stew of eels, freshwater fish and red wine
Bouilli, bouillie	Boiled
Bouilloire	Kettle
Bouillinade	Fish, potato and garlic stew
Bouillon	Broth
Boulangère, à la	Served with onion and potato
Boulangerie	Bakery
Boulaud	Pastry cake with fruit
Boule	Name for a large round loaf
Boule-de-neige	Snowball: sponge in whipped cream or ice-cream in cream
Boulette	Small ball (eg meat ball)
Boulette	Small round herby cows' cheese
Boulette d'Avesnes	Soft strong cows' cheese
Boulette de Cambrai	Ball of soft herby cows' cheese
Boumiane	Stew of tomatoes and aubergines with anchovy garnish
Bouquet	Prawn
Bouquet	Scent

Bouquet	Fragrance or 'nose' of wine
Bouquet garni	Small bunch of herbs
Bouquetière	Served with vegetables
Bourcette	Name for lamb's lettuce
Bourdaine	Apple dumpling
Bourdalue	Poached fruit served hot
Bourdelot	Whole apple in pastry
Bourg, Côtes de, AC	Reds from the Blaye area in Bordeaux
Bourgeois	Middle-ranking
Bourgeoise, à la	Served with carrot, onion and bacon
Bourgeuil, AC	Light red Loire wine
Bourgogne	Burgundy
Bourgogne blanc, AC	Basic burgundy from Chardonnay or Pinot Blanc grapes
Bourgogne rouge, AC	Basic red Burgundy from Pinot Noir grapes
Bourgogne AC	Basic red and white burgundies
Bourguignonne	Red wine sauce with bacon and onion
Bourguignonne, boeuf à la	Beef marinated in red wine, cooked with onions, garlic, mushroom
Bourrache	Borage, a herb
Bourride	Fish soup
Bourse à berger	A name for lamb's lettuce
Boursin	Soft, pasteurized cows' cheese flavoured with herbs and garlic
Boutargue	Paste of dried mullet roes
Bouteille	Bottle
Bouter	Term for wine turned sour

Bouzeron, Bourgogne Aligoté, AC	Fresh white Burgundy from Aligoté grapes
Bouziques	Oysters from Sète
Bouzy	Champagne village producing red wine grapes
Bouzy rouge	Still red wine from Champagne
Bracq	Fresh curd cheese
Braisé, Braisée	Braised
Braisin	Type of haricot bean
Branches, en	Whole leaves, as spinach
Brandade de morue	Purée of salt cod, garlic and oil
Braou	Cabbage and rice soup
Braquet	Provence grape variety
Brasserie	Café or restaurant, usually with snacks, meals, drinks all day
Brébis	Ewe
Brébis d'Oleron	Creamy fresh sheep's cheese
Brébis des Pyrénées	Firm strong sheep's cheese
Bréchet	Breastbone of poultry
Bréjaude	Cabbage and bacon soup
Brème	Bream, freshwater
Brème de mer	Sea bream
Brési	Dried, salted beef or veal
Bresolles	Thinly-sliced meat layered with garlicy stuffing
Bressan	Small conical soft goats' cheese
Bresse Bleu	Cylindrical blue cheese
Bretonne	Creamy white sauce with wine, mushrooms
Bretzel	Pretzel

Brézole	Thick slice of veal
Bricquebec	Flat round mild cows' cheese
Brie	Round flat soft fermented cows' cheese with white rind
Brie, au lait cru	Large, round, fermented cows' cheese of unpasteurised milk
Brigne	Sweet fritter
Brignole	Type of prune
Brigoule	Type of mushroom
Brillat-savarin	Mild rich creamy cows' cheese
Brimbelle	Bilberry flavoured spirit
Brindamour	Tangy herb-coated goats' cheese
Brioche	Soft, sweetish yeast bread
Briolet	Slang term for mediocre wine
Brionne	Name for a custard marrow
Brique du forez	Nutty, loaf-shaped goats' cheese
Broccana	Sausage and veal pate
Broccio	Fresh creamy sheep's cheese
Broche, à la	Spit-roasted
Brochet	Pike
Brochet de mer	Barracuda
Brocheton	Small pike
Brochette	Skewer, kebab
Brocoli	Broccoli
Brosme	Tusk or cusk fish
Brou de noix	Walnut liqueur
Brouet	Broth
Broufado	Beef, onion, anchovy stew
Brouillade	Ingredients stewed or scrambled in oil or butter

Brouillé, Brouillée	Scrambled (as in eggs)
Brouilly, AC	Red wine from one of the ten top Beaujolais villages
Brousse de la Vesubie	Mild creamy ewes' cheese
Brousse du Rove	Mild creamy ewes' cheese
Broutard	Kid
Broutignon	Type of olive
Brouton	Leeks and cabbage in an oil and vinegar sauce
Broye	Type of maize porridge
Brugnon	Nectarine
Brûlé, brûlée	Burned
Brûlot	Flaming brandy
Brun, brune	Brown
Brunoise	Mixture of small diced vegetables, especially root vegetables
Brut	Unrefined
Brut, brute	Unsweetened, as in wine
Bucarde	Cockle
Buccin	Whelk
Bûche	Log, or rolled sponge
Bugey, VDQS	White, red and rosé wines from Savoy
Buglosse	Flower added to salads
Bugnes	Sweet pastry fritters
Buisson, en	In a heap
Bulot	Type of winkle
Burute	A name for black pudding
Buzet, Côtes de, AC	Reds, some white from Southeastern Bordeaux
Byrrh	Quinine-flavoured red wine aperitif

Cabasol	dish of lambs' tripe
Cabécou	Small round goats' or ewes' cheese
Cabécou de Rocamador	Small nutty goats' cheese
Cabernet d'Anjou, AC	Slightly drier rosé from Anjou
Cabernet de Saumur, AC	Fruity rosé from Saumur in Loire
Cabernet franc	Red wine grape, especially grown in Bordeaux and Loire
Cabernet Sauvignon	The claret grape from Bordeaux
Cabessal	Stuffed hare in a red wine sauce
Cabillaud	Cod
Cabot	Name for chub
Caboussat	Wine soup
Cabri	Kid
Cabrières	Mainly rosé wine from Coteaux du Languedoc appellation
Cacahouète	Peanut
Cacao	Cocoa
Cachat	Soft mild creamy ewes' cheese
Cachir	Kosher

Cachuse	Pork and onion stew
Cadillac, AC	Sweetish whites from Bordeaux
Caen, à la	Caen style, usually with calvados
Café	Coffee
Café au lait	Coffee with hot milk
Café complet	Continental breakfast
Café creme	Small coffee with cream
Café deca	Decaffeinated coffee
Café en grains	Coffee beans
Café en poudre	Instant coffee
Café filtre	Filter coffee
Café gallois	Irish coffee
Café glace	Iced coffee
Café moulu	Ground coffee
Café serre	Very strong espresso
Café nature	Coffee without milk
Caghuse	Pork and onion stew
Cagouille	Small snail
Cahlutière	Trawlerman's style: usually with herring
Cahors, AC	Very dark red wine from Lot in the Southwest
Caieu	Type of large mussel
Caille	Quail
Caillé, Caillée	Curdled
Caillé	Milk curds
Caille-botte	Soft creamy fresh cows' cheese, often in rush basket
Cailletot	Name for a young turbot
Caillette	Small quail
Caillette	Pork and vegetable faggot
Caion	A term for pork

Cairanne	Red wine from small Côtes du Rhone village
Caisse	Cashdesk, cashier
Caisse, en	Cooked in a paper case
Cajou	Cashew
Cake	Fruit cake
Calamar	Squid
Calappe	Small crab
Calisson	Marzipan sweet meat
Calmar	Squid
Calva	A term for calvados
Calvados	Normandy cider brandy
Camarguaise	Usually with wine, olives, garlic
Camembert	Soft round fermented cows' cheese
Camomille	Camomile herb
Campagnard	Country-style
Campagne	Country: peasant-style
Campénéac	Strong pressed cows' cheese
Camus	Type of artichoke
Canapé	Bread-based snack
Canard	Duck
Canard sauvage	Wild duck
Canardeau	Duckling
Cancalaise	Usually with cancale oysters
Cancoillotte	Blend of cheese, garlic, wine and butter
Caneton	Duckling
Canette	Female duckling
Canneberge	Name for cranberry
Cannelle	Cinnamon
Canon Fronsac, AC	Good red Bordeaux wine

Canotière	Usually fish poached in white wine
Cantal	Firm yellow Auvergne cows' cheese
Cantareau	Tiny snails in tomato sauce
Canteloupe	Canteloup melon
Cantenac	Bordeaux commune with usually very good red wines
Caouanne	Sea turtle
Capelan	Type of small bony cod, poor cod
Capilotade	Small pieces of poultry or fish
Capitaine	Carp-like saltwater fish
Capoun	Dish of cabbage, sausage and cheese
Câpres	Capers
Caprice des Dieux	Soft very mild cows' cheese
Capsule	Foil or lead cap over cork
Capsule à vis	Screw-top
Capucine	Nasturtium
Carafe	Carafe or small pitcher
Caragoule	Small snail
Caramany	Red and rosé wine, part of Cotes du Roussillon appellation
Caramotte	Prawn
Carbades, VDQS	Red, white and rosé from Roussillon
Carbonnade	Braised dish
Carcasse	Carcass
Cardamome	Cardamom
Carde	Chard
Cardinal	Red wine with cassis
Cardinal	Sauce with lobster and cream
Cardine	Megrim fish

Cardon	Vegetable similar to celery
Cargolade	Snails cooked in wine
Cari	Curry
Carignane	Red wine grape from Midi
Carotte	Carrot
Caroube	Carob
Carpe	Carp
Carpeau	Small carp
Carpillon	Small carp
Carpion	Type of trout
Carrat	Type of sweet pepper
Carré	Square shaped cheese
Carré	Rack (of lamb or veal)
Carré	Square
Carré de Bonneville	Square firm spicy cows' cheese
Carré de Bray	Small square tangy cows' cheese
Carré de l'est	Soft, pasteurised cows' cheese
Carrelet	Plaice
Carte	The main à la carte menu
Carte des vins	Wine list
Cartes de credit	Credit cards
Carvi	Caraway
Caserette	Fresh cheese in a straw basket
Cassate	Assorted ice-creams with glacée fruits
Casse	Pottery stewing pot
Casse rennais	Stew of calf head, trotters in wine
Casse-croute	Snack
Casse-museau	Rock-cake

Casse-noix	Nutcracker
Casserole	Large saucepan
Casseron	A name for cuttlefish
Cassis	Blackcurrant
Cassis, AC	Rosé, white and very few red wines from Provence coast
Cassis, crême de	Blackcurrant liqueur
Cassis, vin blanc	A kir: white wine and blackcurrant liqueur
Cassissine	Blackcurrant stuffing, also blackcurrant candy
Cassolette	Small pottery dish
Cassonade	Soft brown sugar
Cassoulet	Stew of beans, goose, pork and sausage or other meats
Castagnole	Type of sea bream
Castillane	Usually with tomato, potato and onion
Cata	Name for dogfish
Catalan	Usually with tomato, onions, garlic
Catigau	Eel, garlic and red wine stew
Cauchoise	Usually with calvados and cream
Caudière	Type of fish soup
Causses	Blue-mould cows' cheese
Cavallo	Name for a mackerel
Cave	Wine cellar
Cave co-operative	Wine makers co-operative
Caveau	Small cellar, usually for fine wines
Caviar niçois	Mixture of olives, oil, garlic and anchovies

Caviare	Caviar
Caviste	Person in charge of restaurant wine cellar
Cayenne	Red pepper
Cédrat	Type of citrus fruit
Céleri	Celery
Céleri-rave	Celeriac
Cendre	Ash
Cendré d'argonne	Soft, ash-coated cows' cheese
Cendré de champagne	Flat, ash-coated cows' cheese from Champagne
Cendrier	Ashtray
Cendrillon	Cinderella: usually baked in the ashes
Cépage	Term for grape variety
Cèpe	Boletus mushroom
Cereale	Cereal
Cerf	Red deer
Cerfeuil	Chervil
Cerise	Cherry
Cerneau	Green walnut
Cernier	Stone bass
Cérons, AC	Sweet and dry Bordeaux whites
Cervelas	Pork sausage with garlic
Cervelle de canut	Curdled cows' cheese mixed with shallot, herbs and garlic
Cervelles	Brains
Ceteau	Small sole
Cevénole, à la	Usually with chestnuts and mushrooms
Chabi	Strong, soft, conical goats' cheese

Chabichou	Small, strong goats' cheese
Chablis, AC	Burgundy white wine from chardonnay grape
Chablisienne	Usually cooked in white wine from Chablis
Chaboisseau	Type of scorpion fish
Chabot	Name for chub
Chabrol	Soup with added wine
Chachlik	Marinated lamb pieces on skewer
Chai	Wine cellar
Chaigny	Cows' cheese from Orleans
Chair	Flesh
Chaise	Chair
Chalonnaise	Usually with kidneys, mushrooms, truffles, cockscombs
Chalonnaise, côte	Central Burgundy region with red, white and sparkling wines
Chambarand	Mild creamy round cows' cheese
Chamberat	Flat, round fruity cows' cheese
Chambertin, AC	Good red Burgundy wine from Cotes de Nuits
Chambertin-clos de beze, AC	Very good red Burgundy from Cotes de Nuits
Chambolle-musigny, AC	Superior red Burgundy from Cotes de Nuits
Chambourcy	Brand of fresh creamy cows' cheese
Chambrer	To warm a red wine to room temperature
Chamois	Type of antelope
Chamoure	Marrow flan

Champagne	Sparkling wine from strictly-delimited champagne region
Champignon	Edible mushroom
Champigny	Small puff pastry with apricot jam
Champillon	Champagne vineyard near Reims
Champoleon	Hard, skimmed-milk cheese
Champoreau	Black coffee with added liquor
Chanciau	Thick pancake
Chanteclair	Usually stuffed with artichokes and asparagus
Chanterelle	Delicate yellowy mushroom
Chantilly	Whipped cream
Chaource	Cylindrical creamy cows' cheese
Chapeau chinois	Limpet
Chapelure	Breadcrumbs
Chapon	Bread rubbed with oil and garlic
Chapon	Capon chicken, castrated cock
Chapon	Name for scorpion fish
Chaptalisation	Adding of sugar to increase alcohol content
Charbon	Charcoal
Charbon de bois, au	Charcoal-grilled
Charbonné	Goats' cheese dusted with charcoal
Charcuterie	Various pork products (ham, salami, sausage, pate, rillettes)
Charcutièr	Delicatessen specialising in meat products
Chardonnay	White wine grape variety

Charentais	Type of melon
Chariot	Trolley for dessert or cheese
Charlemagne, corton, AC	Very superior white burgundy from Cote de Beaune
Charlotte	Dessert made in mould lined with bread or sponge fingers
Charmes-chambertin, AC	Very good red Burgundy from Cotes de Nuits
Charnu	Full-bodied, as wine
Charol	Goats' cheese from Burgundy
Charolais	Beef cattle from Burgundy
Charolles	Small soft nutty goats' cheese
Chartreuse	Green or yellow brandy liqueur
Chassagne-Montrachet, AC	Superior white, also red, burgundy from Côte de Beaune
Chasselas	White wine grape variety
Chasseur	Usually with wine and mushrooms
Châtaigne	Another name for chestnut
Châtaigne d'eau	Water chestnut
Château	Castle or big house on vineyard
Château-challon, AC	Dry, yellowy white wines from Jura
Châteaubriand	The middle of the beef fillet usually served with potatoes and bearnaise sauce
Châteaumeillant, VDQS	Red, rosé wines from upper Loire
Châteauneuf-du-Pape, AC	Famous Rhone village with full reds, some good whites

Châtillon-en-Diois, AC	Red, white, rosé from the central Rhone valley
Chatouillard	Very thin potato chips
Chatres, pâté de	Partridge paté in pastry crust
Chauchat	Usually fish stewed in wine
Chaud, Chaude	Hot
Chaud-froid	Usually a cold dish of cooked poultry in a white sauce
Chaudé	Plum tart
Chaudeau	Orange tart
Chaudrée	Fish soup or stew with eel
Chaudron	Copper cauldron
Chaume, Quarts de, AC	Sweet white dessert wine from the Loire
Chaumont	Soft, strong conical cows' cheese
Chausson	Pasty or pastry turnover
Chavignol	White wines from small Sancerre commune
Chavignol	Small round goats' cheese
Chayotte	Type of marrow
Cheilly-les maranges, AC	Red, and white Burgundy from Cote de Beaune
Chemise, en	Usually wrapped in, or coated with, another ingredient
Chenas, AC	Red wine from one of the top ten Beaujolais villages
Chenin blanc	White grape variety, especially Loire
Chêne	Oak
Cher	Expensive, dear
Cher, moins	Cheaper, less expensive
Chergouere	Plum pastry
Chétif	Weak (as wine)

Chevaine	Chub fish
Cheval	Horse, horse-meat
Cheval, à	On horseback, or one ingredient atop another
Chevalier-Montrachet, AC	Very good white burgundy from Côtes de Beaune
Cheverny, VDQS	Fresh fruity red, white and rosé from western Loire
Cheveux d'ange	Angel's hair — as in pasta — or very fine strands
Chèvre	Goat, goats' cheese
Chevreau	Kid
Chevret	Small flat goats' cheese
Chevreton d'ambert	Nutty, loaf-shaped goats' cheese
Chevreton de macon	Blue-coated nutty-flavoured goats' cheese
Chevrette	Another name for shrimp
Chevreuil	Venison
Chevreuil, sauce	Usually with red wine and redcurrant jelly
Chevrier	Type of haricot bean
Chevrotin	Goats' cheese, often cone-shaped
Chevrotin des Aravis	Small flat mild goats' cheese
Chevrotin du bourbonnais	Creamy conical goats' cheese
Chevru	Type of well-matured brie
Chez nous, de	Speciality of the house, literally our place
Chicon	Another name for chicory
Chicorée à café	Chicory root
Chicorée frisée	Curly or frizzy edged lettuce
Chiffonade	Thin strips of lettuce, sorrel

Chignin, VDT	White wines from Savoy region
Chinchard	Scad, or horse mackerel
Chinois	Small candied orange
Chinon, AC	Light fruity red from Loire
Chipirons	Another name for squid
Chips	Potato crisps
Chiroubles, AC	Red wine from one of the top ten Beaujolais villages
Chivry	Herb butter especially of chervil or tarragon
Chocolat	Chocolate, also hot chocolate drink
Chocolat à cuire	Cooking chocolate
Chocolat en poudre	Drinking chocolate powder
Choix	Choice, to your choice
Chope	Beer mug
Chorey-les-beaune, AC	Basic Burgundy red from Côte de Beaune
Chorizo	Spicy red sausage
Chorlatte	Stuffed cabbage in pastry
Choron, sauce	Bearnaise sauce with added tomato puree
Chou	Cabbage
Chou	Type of puff pastry
Chou de chine	Chinese leaf
Chou marin	Sea kale
Chou-fleur	Cauliflower
Chou-navet	Swede
Chou-rave	Kohlrabi
Chou-rouge	Red cabbage
Choucroute	Pickled white cabbage
Chouée	Buttered cabbage
Choux	Plural of cabbage

Choux	Puff pastry balls
Choux de bruxelles	Brussels sprouts
Christ-marine	Samphire
Chusclan	Red, white and rosé wines from small Cote du Rhone village
Ciboule	Spring onion
Ciboulette	Chives
Cidre	Cider
Cier de Luchon	Firm strong cows' cheese
Cigale	Type of flat lobster
Cigale, petite	Tiny flat lobster
Cillette	A name for scallop
Cimier	Haunch
Cinsault	Red wine grape, especially Rhone and Midi
Cissac	Bordeaux wine village
Citron	Lemon
Citron pressé	Fresh lemon drink
Citron vert	Lime
Citronnade	Lemon squash
Citronnat	Candied lemon peel
Citronné	Lemon-flavoured
Citronnelle	Lemon liqueur
Citrouille	Pumpkin
CIVC	Committee which rates quality of champagne vineyards
Cive	Term for spring onion
Civelles	Baby eels
Civet	Stew, usually of hare or game
Civette	A name for chives
Clafoutis	Pastry cake usually with cherries

Clair	Clear
Claire	Term for oysters
Clairet	Term for light, fruity red wine
Clairet de moselle	Rosé from Lorraine
Clairette	Type of white wine grape
Clairette de die, AC	Sparkling white from central Rhone valley
Clairette du Languedoc, AC	Light white wine from Midi
Clamart	Usually with peas
Clape, la, VDQS	Red, white, rosé from Midi
Claquebitou	Fresh herb goats' cheese
Clavaire	Type of mushroom
Clémentine	Small orange
Climat	Burgundy term for single vineyard
Climatisée	Air-conditioned
Clitopile	Type of mushroom
Cloche	Bell-shaped cover: glass for cheese, silver for hot dishes
Clos	Vineyard, usually enclosed
Clos de Vougeot, AC	Very good red Burgundy from Côte de Nuits
Clou de Girofle	Clove
Clovisse	Small clam
Clovisse jaune	Small yellow clam
Clupe	Term for small oily fish (sardines or anchovies)
Cooperative	Group of winemakers
Cocherelle	Type of mushroom
Cochon	Pig
Cochon de lait	Suckling pig
Cochonaille	Pork products

Cochonnet	Piglet
Coco	Coconut
Cocotte	Small dish
Coeur	Heart
Coeur de Bray	Heart-shaped fruity cows' cheese
Coeurs de palmier	Palm hearts
Cognac	Brandy only from Cognac region
Coing	Quince
Cointreau	Orange-flavoured liqueur
Colbert	Usually bread-crumbed and fried
Colin	Hake
Colineau	Codling
Collerette	Neck label on bottle
Collerettes, pommes	Very thin slices of fried potato
Collet	Neck (of mutton)
Collioure, AC	Red wine from Roussillon region
Colombard	White wine grape variety
Colombière	Round flat mild cows' cheese
Colombine	Croquette with parmesan and semolina coating
Colvert	Type of wild duck
Comestible	Edible
Commande, sur	As you order it
Commander	To order
Commis	Assistant (to chef or waiter)
Commun	Usual, common
Communard	Red wine with crème de cassis
Commune	Parish, or wine-growing area

Compiègne	Usually with white haricot beans
Complet	Whole (as in bread)
Complet	Full (as in restaurant)
Complet, café	Continental breakfast, coffee or tea with bread, croissant and jam
Composé	Composed of many ingredients
Compote	Stewed fruit
Compotier	Dish for fruit
Compris	Included
Comtadine	Vaucluse-style: often cooked in olive oil and herbs
Comté	Hard round holey cows' cheese
Concassé	Crushed
Concombre	Cucumber
Conde	Type of almond icing
Condrieu, AC	Very good white Rhone wine
Conférence	Conference pear
Confidou	A beef and wine stew
Confiserie	Confectionary
Confit	Crystallised (as fruit)
Confit	Preserved (as goose preserved in its own fat)
Confiture	Jam
Confiture d'orange	Marmalade
Confrérie	Brotherhood (especially of wine lovers)
Congre	Conger eel
Conne	Creamy conical goats' cheese
Conseil	Advice, recommendation
Conseillé	Recommended

Conserve	Preserve
Consommations	Drinks or food consumed in a café or bar
Consommé	Clear soup
Contre-filet	Cut of beef sirloin
Contre-étiquette	Back label (on wine)
Contrex	Still mineral water
Copeau	Shaving, especially of chocolate for decoration
Coq	Cockerel
Coq de bruyère	Wood grouse
Coq de mer	Type of crab
Coque	Shell or husk of nut
Coque	Cockle
Coque	Shell (as in egg)
Coquelet	Cockerel
Coquelicot	Poppy
Coqueret	Strawberry tomato
Coquetier	Eggcup
Coquette, vieille	Type of wrasse
Coquillage	Shellfish
Coquille	Shell (as shellfish)
Coquille St Jacques	Scallop
Coquillettes	Pasta shells
Corail	Coral, as in lobster
Corb	Crowfish, similar sea bass
Corbeau	Type of small sea bass
Corbeille	Basket (as in fruit)
Corbières, AC	Red and rosé wines from Roussillon region
Cordon	Ribbon or band
Cordon bleu	Blue ribbon, originally for lady chefs
Coriandre	Coriander

Coriphene	Dolphinfish, similar to bream
Cornas, AC	Good red from Rhone valley
Corne	Type of walnut
Cornel	Type of cherry
Cornet	Cornet-shape: usually of ham
Cornet	Horn-shaped shellfish
Cornichon	Gherkin
Corse	Tangy blue ewes' cheese
Corton-Charlemagne, AC	Very good white Burgundy From Côte de Beaune
Cosse	Pod (as in pea)
Costières du Gard, AC	Red, rosé and some white from Gard region near Nimes
Coteaux des baux de Provence, VDQS	Red, white, rosé from Provence
Côte	Rib or chop
Côte première	Loin chop
Côte	Slope or hillside
Côte d'Or	Area for good Burgundy reds and whites
Côte de Beaune, AC	Mostly red from nineteen Burgundy communes in Côte d'Or
Côte de Brouilly, AC	Red wine from one of the top ten Beaujolais villages
Côte de Nuits	Burgundy region with mostly red wines
Côte Rôtie, AC	Very good northern Rhone reds
Coteaux	Slopes or hillside vineyard
Coteaux Champenois, AC	Still wines from Champagne region
Coteaux d'Acenis, VDQS	Red, white, rosé from Loire valley

Coteaux de l'Aubance, AC	Dry and medium Loire whites
Coteaux de la Loire, Anjou, AC	Mainly sweet Loire whites
Coteaux de Pierrevert, VDQS	Southern Rhone whites, rosés
Coteaux de Saumur, AC	Sparkling Loire red, white and rosé
Coteaux de l'Ardeche, VDP	Northern Rhone reds and whites
Coteaux du Giennois, VDQS	Red and white from upper Loire
Coteaux du Languedoc, VDQS	Full reds from Midi region
Coteaux du Layon, AC	Sweet whites from central Loire
Coteaux du Tricastin, AC	Full soft Southern Rhone reds
Coteaux du Vendomois, VDQS	Red, white and rosé from upper Loire
Côtelette	Cutlet
Côtes d'Agly, VDN	Sweet whites from Roussillon
Côtes de Bordeaux, première, a	Sweet whites from Bordeaux
Côtes de Castillon,	Decent reds from Bordeaux
Bordeaux supérieure, AC	Supérieure appellation
Côtes de Duras, AC	Reds and whites from near Bergerac
Côtes de Gascogne, VDP	Whites and some red from Southwest
Côtes de Montravel, AC	Sweetish whites from near Bergerac
Côtes de provence, AC	Provence red, rosé and some white

Côtes de Rousillon, AC	Full-bodied reds from Midi
Côtes de Roussillon villages	Red wines with more alcohol than basic Côtes du Roussillon
Côtes du Forez, VDQS	Light reds, rosé from Lyon area
Côtes du Haut-Roussillon	Sweet whites from Southwest
Côtes du Jura, AC	Red, white, rosé from the Jura hills
Côtes du Marmandais, VDQS	Light reds, whites from Eastern France near Bordeaux
Côtes du Rhone, AC	Red, white, rosé from specific villages in Rhone valley
Côtes du Toul, VDQS	Light rosés from Lorraine
Côtes du Ventoux, AC	Red, some white from Southern Rhone
Côtes du Vivarais, VDQS	Red, white, rosé from Western Rhone
Côtes Roannaise, VDQS	Fruity reds from Loire valley
Cotignac	Quince paste
Cotriade	Fish stew with mussels
Cou	Neck
Coucoumelle	Type of mushroom
Coudenou	Large pork sausage
Coudes	Elbow-shaped pasta
Couennes	Rinds (usually of pork)
Couhé-Vérac	Soft, nutty square goats' cheese
Coulandon	Soft fresh cows' cheese
Coulant	Soft, easy drinking wine

Coulemelle	Type of mushroom
Coulibiac	Salmon wrapped in pastry
Coulis	Purée or sauce
Coulommiers	Soft, tangy circular cows' cheese
Coupage, vin de	Blend of weak and strong wine
Coupe	Glass or dish often of ice-cream
Coupe Jacques	Ice-cream with fruit and kirsch
Couperet	Meat cleaver
Courge	General term for gourds
Courgette	Courgette or zucchini
Couronne	Crown
Couronne	Ring-shaped loaf of bread
Courraye	Type of black pudding
Court-bouillon	Poaching broth
Cous-cous	Steamed semolina dish usually with vegetables, chicken or meat
Cousinat	Chestnut soup
Cousinet	A name for cranberry
Cousinette	Soup of spinach, sorrel and lettuce
Couteau	Razor shell clam
Couteau	Knife
Coutellerie	Cutlery
Couvert	Cover charge
Couvert	Place setting
Couverture	Fine chocolate for coating
Crabe	Crab
Crabe enragé	Type of shore crab
Crabe vert	Green-backed shore crab
Crachoir	Spittoon

Cramant	Village in Champagne
Crapaud	Toad
Crapaudine	Spatchcock: chicken, split, flattened and grilled
Craquelin	Cracker or biscuit
Craquelot	Bloater
Craterelle	Type of mushroom
Créat	A name for sturgeon
Crecy	Usually with carrots
Crèmaillère	Hook for hanging pots in chimney
Crémant	Slightly sparkling
Crémant de Cramant	Lightly sparkling champagne from Cramant village
Crème	Cream
Crème	Cream soup
Crème brûlée	Custard with burnt sugar topping
Crème caramel	Custard with caramel bottom
Crème des Vosges	Soft creamy cows' cheese
Crème fleurette	Whipping cream
Crème fouettée	Whipped cream
Crème Fraîche	Lightly soured cream
Crème Patissière	Custard topping or filling for pastry
Crème renversée	Cream caramel, turned upside down
Crème, à la	With cream or in a cream sauce
Crémet	Unsalted, fresh cream cheese
Crémet	Fresh cream cheese mixed with whipped cream and egg white
Crenilabre	Wrasse, similar to sea perch

Créole	Usually with rice, tomato, peppers
Crêpe	Thin pancake
Crépine	Membrane for wrapping sausage
Crépinette	Small sausage
Crépy, AC	Light dry white from Haut-Savoie
Crespeu	Omelette with bacon and potatoes
Cresson	Watercress
Cressonette	Cress
Crête	Crest, often cockscomb
Cretons	Crackling (as in pork)
Creuse	Type of oyster
Creusois	Small hard cows' cheese
Creux	Term for wine without any body
Crevette	Shrimp or prawn
Crevette grise	Brown shrimp
Crevette nordique	Deep-water prawn
Crevette rosé	Common small prawn
Crevette rouge	Large red prawn
Crézancy-Sancerre	Small round goats' cheese
Criadillas	Name for bulls' testicles
Criots-Bâtard-Montrachet, AC	Superior dry white Burgundy From Cote de Beaune
Criquette	Potato pancake
Crispé	Fried bread dumplings
Croissant	Crescent-shaped pastry
Cromesqui	Small battered, deep-fried balls of various ingredients
Croquant	Crunchy
Croque-au-sel	Raw with added salt

Croque-madame	Toasted cheese sandwich with ham and a fried egg
Croque-monsieur	Toasted cheese and ham sandwich
Croquembouche	Usually a tall cone of cream puffs coated with caramelised sugar
Croquet	Small crisp biscuit
Croquette	Small crumbed, fried cylinder, often potato, also other foods
Crottin, de chavignol	Small, hard, round, strong-smelling goats' cheese
Croupion	Parson's nose (as in poultry)
Croustade	Deep case of pastry, bread etc
Croustillant	Crisp, crusty
Croustille	Potato crisp; thin, round, deep fried potato slice
Croûte	Crust or coating
Croûte-au-pot	clear soup, drawn from a pot-au-feu
Croûton	Small piece of fried bread
Crozes Hermitage, AC	Good red and white Rhone wine
Cru	Raw
Cru	Growth, as first growth, second growth wines
Cru bourgeois	Middle-ranking Bordeaux wines
Cru bourgeois supérieur	Better than middle ranking
Cruchade	Maize fritter
Crudités	Raw vegetables usually with dip
Crustaces	Crustacean family

Cuillère	Spoon
Cuillère à café	Teaspoon
Cuisine	Kitchen or cooking
Cuisse	Thigh
Cuisses de grenouille	Frogs' legs
Cuisseau	Leg of veal
Cuisson	Cooking stock
Cuissot	Haunch, especially of venison
Cuit	Cooked
Cuivre	Copper
Cul	Bottom or chump end of joint
Cul-sec	Bottoms up
Cul-blanc	White-tail: small game bird
Culotte de boeuf	Part of beef hindquarter, after sirloin removed
Cumières	Vineyard area of Champagne
Cumin	Cumin
Curcuma	Turmeric
Curé, omelette	Priest's omelette: usually with tuna, cod roes
Cure-dent	Toothpick
Cuve	Wine vat
Cuvé close	Method of making sparkling wine
Cuvée spéciale	Special reserve
Cuvée	The wine in the vat, also a special blending of wine
Cygne	Swan

D'artagnan	Usually with tomatoes, mushrooms and potato croquettes
Dail	Large shellfish
Dame-blanche	Poached pear with ice cream
Dame-jeanne	Demijohn bottle: 5.45 litres
Danoise	Danish-style
Darblay	Thick potato soup
Dard	Dace, freshwater fish
Dariole	Small cylindrical cake
Darne	Thick slice or steak
Dartois	Almond puff pastries, also small pastry snacks usually served hot
Datte	Date
Datte der mer	Small shellfish
Dattier	Type of table grape
Daube	Stew of wine meat/fish/poultry/game, vegetables and herbs
Daubière	Stewpot with tight-fitting lid
Dauphin	Soft, herby cows' cheese
Dauphine, pommes de terre	Deep-fried balls of potato and chou paste
Daurade	Gilt-head bream
Deauvillaise	Usually fish poached with cream and onions
Debarrasser	To clear (as table)

Déboucher	Uncork, open (a bottle)
Décanter	To decant
Décapsuleur	Bottle-opener
Decize	Soft white-rind cows' cheese
Décommandé	Not recommended
Deffarde	Lambs' tripe stew
Dégorgement	Method of removing sediment from champagne
Dégraissé	De-fatted
Degré alcoolique	Degree of alcohol in wine
Dégustation	Tasting
Déjeuner	Lunch
Déjeuner, petit	Breakfast
Délice	Delight, delicious dish
Délice de St Cyr	Small soft creamy cows' cheese
Demain	Tomorrow
Demi	Half
Demi-bouteille	Half bottle
Demi-carapace	Half-shell
Demi-deuil, à la	Usually with white sauce and truffles
Demi-feuillettée	Type of pastry
Demi-glace	Rich, shiny meat sauce
Demi-sec	Half-dry, often half-sweet
Demi-sel	Lightly salted
Demi-sel	Fresh, square cows' cheese
Demi-tasse	Small cup
Demoiselle	Small lobster
Denté	Type of sea bream
Dents-de-lion	A name for dandelion
Derobé	Skinned, shelled
Dés, en	Diced
Désagréable	Unpleasant

Desossé	Boned
Dessert	Dessert
Deuxième cru	Quality classification below grand cru and premier cru
Dévisser	To unscrew
Dézize-les-maranges, AC	Light, red, white from Burgundy
Diable de mer	A name for monkfish
Diable, à la	Devilled, spicy
Diablotins	Spicy toasted cheese squares
Diane	Usually with creamy black pepper sauce
Dieppoise	Usually with white wine, mussels, crayfish tails
Digestif	After dinner drink
Dijonnaise	Usually with mustard sauce, or with blackcurrants, or cassis
Dinde	Turkey hen
Dindon	Turkey cock
Dindonneau	Young turkey
Diner	Dinner, also to dine
Diot	Pork and vegetable sausage
Diplomat	Usually with kidney, sweetbreads and mushrooms
Diplomat	Cold fruit and sponge pudding
Divers	Varied
Dobule	Type of chub
Dodine	Boned, stuffed piece of duck or other poultry
Dôle	Red wine grape variety
Dom Perignon	Monk who invented champagne
Domaine	Wine estate or vineyard

Dominique	Usually with wine, mushrooms, cream and a cheese sauce
Donzelle	Small eel-shaped seafish
Dorade	Red sea bream
Doré	Golden
Doria	Usually with cucumber garnish
Dormeur	A type of crab
Dornecy	Strong, dry goats' cheese
Dorure	Glaze of egg-yolk
Dosage	Sugar added to champagne
Douarnenez	Usually with sardines
Double	Double
Douce	Soft, sweet, mild
Doucette	Name for lamb's lettuce
Doux	Sweet
Doyenné	Type of pear
Dragée	Pastel-coloured sugar almond
Droit de douane	Duty
Droit, exempté de	Duty-free
Dubarry	Usually with cauliflower, cheese
Dubois, oeufs	Scrambled eggs and lobster
Dubonnet	Bitter-sweet aperitif
Duchesse, pommes	Mashed potatoes with egg and butter
Ducs	Soft cylindrical cows' cheese
Dugléré	Usually with tomatoes, herbs, onions, white wine
Dur	Hard
Dur, vin	Hard wine: usually caused by too much tannin
Duroc	Sautéed whole new potatoes
Duxelles	Chopped mushrooms, shallots sautéed in butter

Eau	Water
Eau de robinet	Tap water
Eau de vie	Clear alcoholic spirit
Eau douce	Fresh water
Eau minéral sans gaz	Still mineral water
Eau minérale avec gaz	Sparkling mineral water
Eau non potable	Undrinkable water
Eau potable	Drinkable water
Écaille d'huitre	Oyster shell
Écaillé	Shelled or scaled
Écarlate, a l'	Pickled (usually meat)
Échalote	Shallot
Échaudé	Pastry bun
Échaudé	Scalded
Échezeaux, AC	Decent burgundy reds from Côte de Nuits
Échine	Chine (usually of pork)
Échiquier	Chequered pattern
Emporter	To take-away
Échirlette, à la	Potatoes in goose or pork fat
Échourgnac	Small, round yellow cows' cheese
Éclade	Stew of mussels cooked over pine needles
Éclair	Small chou pastry, usually iced
Éclanche	Term for shoulder, especially of mutton

Écorce	Peel or bark
Écossaise	Scottish-style
Écrevisse	Crayfish
Écuelle	Bowl, porridge bowl
Écureuil	Squirrel
Edam	Red coated spherical cheese
Édelzwicker	Alsace white wine
Égal, à	Equal to
Églantine	Wild rose jam, also liqueur from Alsace
Églefin	A name for haddock
Égrugeoir	Grinder, mill for salt or pepper
Eledone	Tiny octopus
Emballer	To wrap
Embeurré	Buttered
Éméché	Tipsy
Émincé	Thinly sliced
Émincé	Dish made of thin-sliced left-over meat
Émissole	Spotted shark
Émondé	Blanched
Emporter	To take-away
En portefeuille	Wrapped inside another ingredient
En réclame	Special offer, promotion
En retard	Late
Encastré	Set in
Enchaud	Pork loin cooked with trotters and garlic
Encore de	Some more
Encornet	Squid
Encre	Ink (as in octopus)
Endaubage	Slang term for tinned meat

Endive	Chicory
Entier, entière	Whole
Entolome	Type of mushroom
Entrammes	Smooth mild orange-coated cows' cheese
Entre-Deux-Mers, AC	White wines from Bordeaux
Entrecôte	Rib steak
Entrée	Usually the main course but can be dish before the meat course
Entremets	Usually dessert, but can mean dish served between courses
Épaule	Shoulder
Éperlan	Smelt
Epernay	Important champagne town
Epi	Type of crusty long bread loaf
Épice	Spice
Épicerie	Grocer's shop
Épinards	Spinach
Épine d'hiver	Type of pear
Épine-vinette	Barberries, similar capers
Épinoche	Small freshwater fish
Époisses	Small strong cheese cured with marc de Bourgogne
Équilibré	Well-balanced (esp. wine)
Équille	Sand eel
Ercé	Firm strong cows' cheese
Ériphie	Type of crab
Ermite	Very old wild boar
Ervy-le-Châtel	Small firm, conical cows' cheese

Escabeche	Cold cooked and marinated fish
Escalope	Thin slice of meat or fish
Escargot	Snail
Escargot de mer	Small shellfish
Escarole	Salad green, type of lettuce
Espadon	Swordfish
Espagnole	Spanish-style: usually with tomato, onion, peppers
Esprot	Sprat
Esquinado	A name for spider crab
Essence	Essence or extract
Est	East
Estival	Related to summer
Estoficado	Dried, flattened cod
Estomac	Stomach
Estouffade	Stewed joint of meat
Estragon	Tarragon
Esturgeon	Sturgeon
Étain	Tin
Été	Summer
Étiquette	Label
Étoile	Star
Etorki	Firm strong sheep's cheese
Étouffé, étoffé	Stuffed
Étourdeau	A young capon
Étrille	Small crab
Étuvé, étouffée	Stewed or braised, also steamed
Evian	Still mineral water
Excelsior	Small mild soft cows' cheese
Exécrable	Awful, abominable
Explorateur	Mild rich creamy cows' cheese

Express	Espresso
Extra-sec	Very dry
Extrait	Essence, extract

Façon, à la	In the way of, manner of
Fagot	Meatball
Fagoue	Sweetbreads
Faim	Hunger
Faim, avoir	To be hungry
Faine	Beechnut
Faisan	Pheasant
Faisandé	Gamey, highly flavoured
Faisandeau	Young pheasant
Faiselle	Pot for draining cheese, also term for drained curd cheese
Fallette	Mutton stuffed with vegetables and bacon
Falue	Sweetened pancake
Famille	Family-style
Fanchonette	Meringue
Fanes	Tops of root vegetables, often used for soups
Fanfre	Fish similar to mackerel
Faon	Fawn
Far	Buckwheat mixture, sweet or savoury
Farandole	Usually a fancy dish or dessert
Farce	Stuffing
Farci, farcie	Stuffed
Farcidure	Vegetable dumpling
Farée	Stuffed cabbage

Farigoule	Name for wild thyme
Farigoulette	Wild thyme
Farine	Flour
Farinette	Type of pancake
Faséole	Kidney bean
Fassum	Cabbage stuffed with bacon, rice, sausagemeat and onions
Faugères, AC	Red, white, rosé from Languedoc
Fausse	False
Fausse limande	Flatfish or scaldfish
Fausse tortue, potage	Mock turtle soup, made of calf's head
Fausse-sole	Sand-dab
Fauve	Wild animal
Faux	False
Faux-café	Decaffeinated coffee
Faux-filet	Cut of beef fillet
Favorite, à la	Usually with artichoke, mushroom and potato cakes
Favouille	Small crab
Fèche	Dried pork livers
Fécule	Starch
Fenouil	Fennel
Fenouil marin	Samphire
Fenouillette	Fennel seed liqueur
Féouse	Bacon and onion flan
Fera	Type of lake salmon
Ferchuse	Pork liver, lungs, heart in garlic and red wine
Fermé	Closed
Fermeture	Closing
Fermeture annuelle	Annual closing, annual holidays

Fermeture, hebdomadaire	Weekly closing day
Fermier	From the farm
Fermière, à la	Usually with lots of vegetables
Ferrecapienne	Type of fish soup
Fête	Party
Feu	Fire
Feuillantine	Small pastry
Feuille	Leaf
Feuille de Dreux	Soft round fruity cows' cheese
Feuilletée	Puff pastry case
Feuilleton	Thin slices of veal/pork with stuffing
Fève	Broad bean
Féverole	Type of small broad bean
Fiatole	Pomfret
Ficelle	Long thin loaf
Fichu	A wrapping or coating
Fiefs Vendeens, VDQS	Reds, whites, rosés from Nantes region
Fiéle, fiéla	Name for eel
Figon	Small fig
Figue	Fig
Figue de barbarie	Prickly pear
Figue de mer	Sea-fig, small sea creature
Figue-caque	Name for persimmon
Filet	Fillet of meat or fish
Fillette	Term for a half-bottle
Fin	Fine
Fin de serie	Bin-end
Fin de siècle	Soft, creamy cows' cheese
Fine	Brandy

Fine	Fine
Fine de claire	Type of oyster
Fines herbes	Mixed chopped herbs
Finte	Name for shad
Fistuline	Type of mushroom
Fitou, AC	Rich red wine from Roussillon
Fixe	Fixed, set
Fixin, AC	Good red burgundy from the Côte de Nuits
Flageolet	Green kidney bean
Flagnarde	Thick sweet pancake
Flamande	Flemish-style, often with cabbage, onions or potato
Flambé	Flamed
Flamiche	Cheese and leek tart
Flamri	Semolina pudding served with fruit
Flamusse	Sweet omelette
Flan	Name for creme caramel
Flan	Open egg custard tart
Flanchet	Flank
Flandre	A name for flounder
Flet	Flounder or flat fish
Flétan	Halibut
Fleur	Flower
Fleur de Decauville	Soft cows' cheese from île-de-france
Fleur de maïs	Cornflour
Fleurie, AC	Red wine from one of the ten leading Beaujolais villages
Fleuron	Small puff pastry garnish
Flie	A clam
Flip	Cider topped with flaming spirit

Floc de Gascogne	Grape juice and armagnac aperitif
Flocon	Flake
Flocon de maïs	Cornflake
Flognarde	Thick sweet pancake
Florentine	Usually served on spinach
Floute	Tiny potato dumpling
Flûte	Long, slim loaf of bread
Foie	Liver
Foie de veau	Calf's liver
Foie gras	Delicacy of force-fed goose or duck liver
Foie-de-boeuf	Ox liver
Foin	Hay
Foin d'artichaut	Centre of artichoke
Foin, jambon au	Ham boiled in hay
Folle	Frivolous
Folle-blanche	White wine grape variety
Fond	Base
Fond d'artichaut	Artichoke bottom
Fondant	Melting
Fonds	Stock
Fonds de cuisine	Basic cooking stocks
Fondu	Melted
Fondu aux raisin	Grape-seed coated cows' cheese
Fondue Bourguignonne	Hot oil for dipping small pieces of steak
Fondue au fromage	Melted cheese with wine and kirsch for dipping bread
Fontainebleu	Fresh rich creamy cows' cheese
Fontine	Firm yellow holey cows' cheese

Forestière	Usually with mushrooms, bacon and potatoes
Fort(e)	Strong
Fou	Crazy
Fouasse	Term for cakes and pastries
Foudre	Large barrel
Fouet	Whisk
Fouettée	Whipped or whisked
Fougassette	Orange cake
Fougère	Edible fern shoots
Fougeru	Soft cows' cheese wrapped in ferns
Foulque	Coot
Four	Oven
Four, au	Baked or roasted
Fourchette	Wishbone
Fourchette	Fork
Fourderaine	Sloe liqueur
Fourme	Type of cheese, usually blue-veined
Fourme d'Ambert	Cylindrical blue cows' cheese
Fourme de Montbrison	Cylindrical, firm cows' cheese
Fourme de Pierre sur Haute	Tangy blue-mould cows' cheese
Fourme de salers	Firm, nutty yellow cows' cheese
Fourré	Stuffed or filled
Fraîche	Fresh or uncured, as cheese
Fraîche, frais	Fresh or cool, refreshing
Frais, vin	Cool (wine)
Fraise	Strawberry
Fraise de bois	Wild strawberry
Fraise de veau	Membrane encasing calf's intestine

Framboise	Raspberry
Franc-de-goût	Clean-tasting
Francolin	Game bird
Frangipane	Confectionary custard with crushed macaroons
Franquette	Type of walnut
Frappé	Cool, iced drink
Frappé	Iced, or served with crushed ice
Fréchure	Stew of pig's lung
Frémir	To simmer
Frêne	Ash tree: shoots used in salads
Frénette	Cool drink made from leaves of ash tree
Fressure	Pluck or offal, usually of pig
Fretin	Fish fry, spawn
Freux	Rook
Friand	Fruity (as wine)
Friande	Small pastry
Friandise	Sweet or petit four
Fricadelle	Deep-fried ball, usually of meat
Fricandeau	Large slice of fish cooked in the style of meat
Fricandeau	Topside of veal
Fricassée	Light creamy stew, usually chicken or veal
Fricassin	Calf's intestinal membrane in wine sauce
Fricaude	Stewed pigs' offal
Frigolet	Name for wild thyme
Frinault	Small, soft cows' cheese often ash-coated
Frisée	Curly lettuce
Frit, frite	Fried

Frites	Potato chips
Fritot	Fritter
Frittons	Deep-fried pieces of pork or goose
Friture	Platter of fried-food, especially small fish
Frivolle	Fritter
Froid, froide	Cold
Fromage	Cheese
Fromage à la crème	Cream cheese
Fromage à la pie	Fresh unfermented cows' cheese
Fromage à tartiner	Cheese spread
Fromage blanc	Fresh cream cheese, often eaten with fruit
Fromage de tête	Brawn
Fromage du Curé	Small strong square cows' cheese
Fromage fermier	Cheese made on the farm
Fromage fondu	Processed cheese
Fromage fort	Fermented cheese blended with herbs and brandy
Fromage frais	Liquid fresh cream cheese, used like sour cream
Fromage laitier	Cheese made by dairy or factory
Fromage maigre	Low-fat cheese
Fromagée	With added cheese
Fromaget	Cheesecake
Froment	Wheat
Fronsac, AC	Full reds from Bordeaux
Frontignan	Sweet fortified wine from Herault
Fronton, VDQS	Red and rosé from South-western France

Fruit	Fruit
Fruit de la passion	Passion fruit
Fruité	Fruity
Fruiterie	Greengrocer's shop
Fruits de mer	Seafood
Fuisse, Macon, AC	White burgundy from one of Macon's listed villages
Fumé blanc	Sauvignon grape
Fumé, fumée	Smoked
Fumer	To smoke
Fumet	Cooking stock, especially fish
Fût	Wine cask: 400 litres

Gadelle	Gooseberry
Gaillac, AC	Still and sparkling whites from Southwestern France, also some reds
Galabart	Large black pudding
Galantine	Jellied mould of meat, fish or poultry
Galathée	Type of freshwater crayfish
Galette	Thick pancake or flat pastry
Galette de la Chaise-dieu	Flat, round nutty goats' cheese
Galicien	Pistachio sponge cake
Galimafrée	Peasant stew in rough wine
Galinette	Tub gurnard, tasty long thin seafish
Galopin	Thick pancake with breadcrumbs
Gamay	Red wine grape variety
Gamba	Large prawn
Ganga	Type of grouse
Gaperon	Soft round cows' cheese with garlic flavour
Gapon	Garlic flavoured cows' cheese
Garbure	Bean soup with vegetables, traditionally finished with wine
Garciaux	Small smoked eels
Gard, VDP	Red, white and rosé from Southern France

Gardon, gardon rouge	Roach
Garenne	Rabbit warren, also a name for wild rabbit
Gargameu	Name for a tomato omelette
Garni	Garnished
Garniture	Garnish
Gascogne, beurre de	Type of garlic butter
Gasconnade	Lamb with anchovies and garlic; also ham and parsley garnish
Gastrochère	Small shellfish
Gat	Name for a dogfish
Gâteau	Cake, tart or loaf
Gatis	Cheese-filled brioche
Gaudes	Type of polenta or maize meal
Gaufre	Waffle
Gaufrette	Potato crisp or chip
Gay-lussac	French chemist who gave name to alcohol measuring system
Gazeifié	Carbonated wine
Gazeux, gaseuse	Carbonated
Geai	Jay: eaten when young
Gebie	Small shellfish
Gélatine	Gelatine
Gelée	Jelly on aspic
Gelinotte	Type of grouse
Gendarme	Name for a pickled herring
Genepy	Herbal liqueur
Genevoise, sauce	Sauce of fish stock, red wine wine and anchovy essence
Genièvre	Gin
Genièvre	Juniper berry

Génisse	Heifer
Génoise, à la	Usually with tomato sauce
Gentiane	Liqueur from gentian flowers
Gentil	Alsace name for Riesling grape
Gentilhomme, potage	Lentil and game soup
Georgette, pommes	Baked potato with crayfish tails
Gérant	Manager
Gérardmer	Thick round soft golden cows' cheese
Germe de soja	Soya beansprouts
Germon	Albacore tuna
Géromé	Spicy soft round golden cows' cheese often covered with fennel
Gésier	Gizzard
Gevrey-Chambertin, AC	Very good red burgundy from Côte de Nuits
Gewürztraminer	Alsace white wine grape
Gex	Large round blue cows' cheese
Gibelotte	Stew, usually of rabbit
Gibier	Game
Gien	Small firm goats' or cows' cheese, leaf-wrapped
Gigondas, AC	Full reds and rosés from small Rhone village
Gigot	Leg of lamb or mutton
Gigouret	Pig's head stewed in wine
Gigue	Haunch, especially venison
Gingembre	Ginger
Girasol	Name for a Jerusalem artichoke

Girelle	Wrasse
Girofle	Clove
Girolle	Type of mushroom
Gironde	Bordeaux river estuary
Gîte	Shin of beef
Givré	Frosted
Givry, AC	Red or white Burgundy from Côte Chalonnaise
Glaçage	Icing
Glace	Glaze (as sauce)
Glace, glacier	Ice-cream
Glace	Ice
Glacé, glacée	Frozen, iced
Glaçon	Ice-cube
Gnocchi	Dumplings, usually potato or chou paste
Gnocchi, à la Romaine	Semolina dumplings with grated cheese
Gnôle	A term for brandy
Gobelet	Goblet
Gobie	Goby fish
Godaille	Selection of small fish, especially for soup
Godfiche	Name for a scallop
Godiveau	Veal stuffing
Gogue, goguette	Small pork sausage
Golmotte	Type of mushroom
Gombaut	Okra
Goret	Small pig
Goudale	Wine added to soup
Gouerre	Cake or tart
Gouffé	Garnish of mashed potato, asparagus and mushrooms
Gougère	Choux pastry with cheese

Gougnette	Large sweet fritter
Goujon	Small freshwater fish
Goujon	Small strip of fish, usually coated and deep-fried
Gourilos	Endive shoots
Gourmand	One over-fond of food, a greedy person
Gourmandise	Sweetmeat
Gourmet	Connoisseur of food
Gournay	Small round cured cows' cheese on straw
Gournay frais	Soft fresh salty round cows' cheese
Gousse	Pod
Gousse d'ail	Clove of garlic
Goût	Taste
Goût, mauvais	Bad-taste, off-taste (as wine)
Goût de rancio	Sour taste of wine that is off
Goûter	To taste
Goutte	A drop
Goyave	Guava
Goyère	Tart of strong cured cheese and cream
Graçay	Small goats' cheese in charcoal
Grain	Berry or bean
Grain de raisin	Grape
Graine	Seed
Grains de café	Coffee beans
Graisse	Fat, lard
Graisse de rognon	Suet
Graisserons	Potted pork
Gramolate	A name for sorbet
Grand cru	A great growth, as in wine

Grand cru bourgeois exceptionelle	Best of middle-ranked bordeaux
Grand Marnier	Orange brandy liqueur
Grand ordinaire	General term for burgundies
Grand Roussillon, AC	Red, white and rosé from Midi
Grand, grande	Great, large
Grande marque	Indicates one of the sixteen major champagne houses
Grandeur	Size
Grands-échezeaux, AC	Very good red Burgundies from Côte de Nuits
Granité	Granular water ice
Grappe	Grape-pip covered cheese
Gras, grasse	Fatty
Gras-double	Ox-tripe
Grasset	Thinly sliced beef flank
Grataron d'arèches	Round tangy goats' cheese
Gratin	Grilled dish, often with breadcrumbs and cheese
Gratiné, gratinée	Dish grilled or served with toasted cheese and breadcrumbs
Gratte-cul	Rosehip
Grattons	Small pieces of crackling
Gratuit, gratuite	Free
Gratuité	Tip
Gravenche	Type of salmon trout
Graves supérieur, AC	Strong, medium-dry to sweet Bordeaux whites
Graves, AC	Good reds and whites from Bordeaux area with very gravelly soil
Gravette	Type of flat oyster

Grecque, à la	Greek-style; usually with oil, coriander and herbs
Grelot	Type of onion
Gremille	Small freshwater fish
Grenache	Type of grape variety, usually for rosé and red blends
Grenade	Pomegranate
Grenadine	Red syrup, originally of pomegranate
Grenadins	Small thick piece of meat or poultry
Grenoblois	Walnut cake
Grenobloise, à la	Usually fish fried in butter, with capers and lemon
Grenouille	Frog
Grenouille, cuisses de	Frogs' legs
Grenouilles	One of better Chablis vineyards
Gressin	Breadstick
Gribiche	Usually cold sauce with egg, capers, gherkin
Grignan	Herbal liqueur
Grignaudes	Deep-fried pork cubes
Grignon	End of loaf, dry crust
Grignoteries	Nibbles, little snacks
Grillade	Grill
Grillade	Grilled food
Grillé, grillée	Grilled or toasted
Grillettes	Crispy pieces of pork or duck
Griotte	Type of cherry
Gris	Light rosé wine
Gris de lille	Pungent salty cows' cheese with pinkish rind
Gris, grise	Grey

Griset	Black bream
Grisette	Type of mushroom
Grisotte	Type of mushroom
Grive, pâté de	Thrush pâté
Grolleau	Grape variety especially in Anjou for rosés
Grondin	Gurnard fish, tasty long thin sea fish
Grondin galinette	Tub gurnard
Grondin gris	Grey gurnard
Grondin imbragio	Streaked gurnard
Grondin lyre	Piper fish
Gros mollet	Name for lumpfish
Gros pain	Large loaf of bread
Gros plant	Variety of white wine grape
Gros Plant, pays Nantais, VDQS	Very dry white Loire wine
Gros sel	Coarse rock or sea salt
Gros suisse	Large round unsalted goats' cheese
Gros vert	Table grape
Gros, grosse	Big
Gros-blanquet	Type of pear
Groseille	Redcurrant
Groseille à maquereau	Gooseberry
Groseille de cheval	A name for cranberry
Groslot	Grape variety, usually for rosés
Grosse crevette	Prawn
Grosse palourde	Large clam
Grosseur	Size
Grou	Buckwheat fritter
Grouin d'âne	Dandelion

Grouse	Grouse
Gruau	Grain
Gruau d'avoine	Oatmeal
Gryphée	Portuguese oyster
Guenille	Fritter, often potato
Guerbigny	Spicy heartshaped cows' cheese
Guéret	Small hard cows' cheese
Guigne	Type of cherry
Guignette	Name for a sandpiper
Guignette	Name for a winkle
Guignolet	Cherry brandy
Guillaret	Type of pastry
Guimaive, pâté de	Marshmallow sweet
Guimauve	Marshmallow plant
Guitare	Type of skate
Gulyas	Goulash of beef, paprika
Gymnètre	Type of Meditteranean flat fish
Gyrole	Type of mushroom

Haché, hachée	Minced, chopped
Haché, steack/biftek	Hamburger
Hachis	Minced meat
Hachis parmentier	Shepherd's pie
Hachua	Ham stewed with onions and sweet peppers
Haddock	Smoked haddock
Halbran	Young wild duck
Halicot	Stew usually of mutton
Hareng	Herring
Hareng blanc	Salted herring
Hareng roulé	Rollmop herring
Hareng salé	Salted herring
Hareng saur	Whole salted, smoked herring
Haricot	Dried bean
Haricot beurre	Butter bean
Haricot blanc	Dried white haricot bean
Haricot d'espagne	Runner bean
Haricot de mer	Bean clam
Haricot grimpant	Runner bean
Haricot jaune	Butter bean
Haricot rouge	Red kidney bean
Haricot vert	French string bean
Harissa	Spicy sauce served with couscous
Hase	Female rabbit, hare

Hatelet	Skewer
Haut, haute	High
Haut-Bénauge, AC	Dry, medium and sweet whites from Entre-Deux-Mers in Bordeaux
Haut-Medoc, AC	Good to very good reds from Bordeaux
Haut-Montravel, AC	Reds and whites from Bergerac
Haut-Poitou, VDQS	Light reds from Loire valley
Hauteluce	Small Savoy goats' cheese
Helville	Type of mushroom
Hénon	A name for cockle
Hérault	Highly-productive wine-growing region in Southern France
Herbe	Herb
Hère	Young stag
Hérisson	Hedgehog
Hermitage, AC	Good, often very good reds and whites from Northern Rhone
Hêtre	Beech tree
Hirondelle	Swallow
Hiver	Winter
Hochepot	Very mixed soup of pork, beef, mutton, cabbage and vegetables
Hochequeue	Wagtail
Hollandais	Dutch
Hollandaise, sauce	Sauce of butter, egg, lemon, wine and vinegar
Holstein, veau	Veal with fried eggs and anchovies
Homard	Lobster

Homardin	With added lobster
Homère, crème de	Egg custard with honey, wine, cinnamon and lemon
Hongroise	Hungarian, usually with paprika
Hors d'age	Very mature spirit
Hors d'oeuvre	Starter or pre-meal nibble
Hospices de Beaune	Site of famous annual Burgundy wine auction
Hôte	Guest
Hôte	Landlord, patron
Hôte, table d'	The patron's set menu
Hôtel	Hotel, large public building
Hôtelière	Usually with parsley butter
Hôtellerie	Inn
Hôtesse	Hostess
Houblon	Hop
Houblon, jet de	Hopshoot
Houx	Holly liqueur
Houx	Holly
Huile	Oil
Huile d'arachide	Groundnut oil
Huile d'oillette	Poppyseed oil
Huile d'olive	Olive oil
Huile d'olive vierge	Virgin olive oil
Huile de noix	Walnut oil
Huile de soja	Soya bean oil
Huile de tournesol	Sunflower seed oil
Huître	Oyster
Huître creuse	Rough-shelled introduced oyster
Huître de parc	Cultivated oyster
Huître en écaille	Oyster on the shell
Huître plate	Flat round native oyster

Huîtrier	Oyster-catcher bird
Huppemeau	Large round soft cows' cheese, similar brie
Hure de porc	Brawn
Hydne	Type of mushroom
Hydromel	Honey, mead and water
Hypocras	Spiced, sugared red wine
Hysope	Hyssop herb

Igname	Yam
Igny	Round flat pressed cows' cheese
Île flottante	Poached egg white floating in custard
Île-de-France	The region around Paris
Imbuvable	Undrinkable
Imam bayeldi	Aubergine, tomato, onion stewed in oil
Impératrice	Empress style: usually based on rice, cream and fruit
Impériale	Six litre bottle, especially Bordeaux
Impériale	Usually very elaborate presentation, often truffled
Inchville	Small soft white cows' cheese
Indienne	Usually with curry sauce and rice
Infusion	Herb tea
Inmangeable	Inedible
Insipide	Tasteless
Irancy, AC	Red or rosé from Northern Burgundy
Iraty	Firm strong sheeps' cheese
Irlandaise	Irish-style
Irouléguy, AC	Red, white, rosé from Pyrennées
Isigny	Town famous for cheese, butter

Issues	Pluck or offal
Ive	Type of chive
Ivre	Drunk, intoxicated
Izard	Type of antelope
Izarra	Herbal liqueur

Jacque	Apple pancake
Jalousie	Small pastry
Jambon	Ham
Jambon blanc	Cooking ham, cooked ham
Jambon cru	Cured ham eaten raw
Jambon de Bayonne	Cured and smoked ham from Bayonne
Jambon de pays	Smoked, cured country ham
Jambon de York	Cooked, sliced ham
Jambonette	Dried pork sausage
Jambonneau	Whole small ham
Jambonneau	Type of mussel
Jardinière	Garden-style, with vegetables
Jardins de la France, VDP	Red, white, rosé from Loire valley
Jarnac	Sponge cake with meringue and cognac
Jarret	Shin or knuckle
Jasnières, AC	Rare Loire white, can be very good
Jaune	Type of mushroom
Jaune	Yellow
Jaune d'oeuf	Egg yolk
Jereboam	Double magnum: four bottles
Jesse	Freshwater fish
Jesuite	Small almond pastry
Jésus	Type of pork sausage

Jet de houblon	Hopshoot
Joël	Type of sandsmelt
Joinville	Usually shrimps, mushrooms and truffles in a cream sauce
Jonchée	Fresh creamy cows' or goats' or sheep's cheese, presented in a rush basket
Jotte	A name for chard
Joue	Cheek
Jour	Day
Joyeuses	Sheep's testicles
Jubilee, cerises	Cherries flamed in kirsch
Judru	Burgundy pork sausage
Juif, juive	Jewish
Juliénas, AC	Red wine from one of the top ten Beaujolais villages
Julienne	Ling
Julienne	Thin strips usually of vegetables
Jura	Eastern France wine region for red, white, rosé and sparkling
Jurançon, AC	Sweet white from Southwest
Jurançon sec, AC	Dry white from Southwest
Jurassienne	Jura-style, often with ham, onion and sorrel
Jus	Juice
Jus de viande	Gravy
Jus, au	Meat or poultry cooked in its own juices
Juter	To baste
Juteux, juteuse	Juicy

Kaki	Persimmon
Kalerei	Brawn of pig's trotters, tails and ears
Kari	Curry
Ketchup aux tomates	Tomato sauce
Kiev	Deep-fried chicken, stuffed with garlic-butter
Kik'a farz	Buckwheat pudding
Kir	White wine with blackcurrant liqueur
Kirsch	Wild black cherry spirit
Kougloff, Kougelhopf	Brioche ring with dried fruits, nuts
Kouign-amann	Rich buttery Breton loaf
Koulibiac	Another name for coulibiac of salmon and rice in pastry
Kummel	Caraway seed liqueur
— bouille	Tangy, red-speckled cows' cheese
— mothe-St-Héray	Small round goats' cheese

Labre	Wrasse fish, similar to sea perch
Lac	Lake
Lache	Very small sea fish
Lactaire	Type of mushroom
Ladoix-Serigny, AC	Burgundy wine commune, mostly reds in Côte de Nuits
Laguiole	Large round tangy cows' cheese
Lait	Milk
Lait barratté	Buttermilk
Lait de coco	Coconut milk
Lait de poule	Eggnog
Lait demi-écremé	Semi-skimmed milk
Lait écremé	Skimmed milk
Lait entier	Full cream milk
Lait sterilisé	Long-life milk
Lait, petit	Whey
Laitages	Dairy products
Laitance	Fish roe
Laiterie	Dairy
Laitue	Lettuce
Laitue beurrée	Round lettuce
Laitue romaine	Cos lettuce
Lalande de Pomerol, AC	Good to very good reds from Bordeaux commune
Lambeau	Small shred of meat

Lame	Knife-blade: a very thin slice
Lamie	Porbeagle shark
Lampée	A swig (of wine)
Lamprillon	Small lamprey fish
Lamproie	Lamprey fish
Lamproie marine	Sea-lamprey
Lançon	Sand eel
Landaise, à la	Usually with goose fat and pine kernels
Langouste	Spiny lobster
Langoustine	Scampi, Dublin Bay prawn
Langres	Small strong conical cows' cheese
Langue	Tongue
Langue de boeuf	Ox tongue
Langue de chat	Long thin boudoir biscuit
Languedoc	Southern province producing large volume of red and rosé wines
Languedocienne	Usually with tomato, aubergine and garlic
Languier	Smoked pigs' tongue
Lapereau	Young rabbit
Lapin	Rabbit
Lard	Pork fat
Lardon	Rasher of bacon
Large	Broad
Larron d'ors	Strong tangy square cows' cheese
Laruns	Firm strong sheep's cheese
Latour	Mackerel shark
Latour de France, AC	Red and white wine from Roussillon
Laudun	Good red, white, rosé from Côtes du Rhone appellation

Laumes	Small firm conical goats' cheese
Laurier	Laurel tree
Laurier, feuille de	Bayleaf
Laval	Smooth, firm cows' cheese
Lavaret	Freshwater fish similar to salmon
Lèche	Very thin slice
Léger	Light (as wine)
Légume	Vegetable
Légume primeur	Spring vegetable
Lentille	Lentil
Lentement	Slowly
Lent, lente	Slow
Lépiote	Type of mushroom
Les orrys	Large round strong cows' cheese
Les riceys	Small, soft round cows' cheese
Levadou	Stew of pigs' lungs
Levraut	Young hare
Levroux	Mild, nutty goats' cheese
Levure	Yeast
Lézard	Lizard fish
Liaison	Thickening for sauce
Liard, en	Usually very thin round sliced fried potatoes
Liche	Type of amberjack, similar tuna
Lie	The lees or sediment of wine
Lié	Bound or thickened, as sauce
Liégoise	Usually with juniper or gin
Liégoise, café	Iced coffee with cream and ice-cream

Lieu	Place
Lieu jaune	Pollack fish
Lieu noir	Coley
Lièvre	Hare
Liève de mer	Lumpfish
Ligueil	Soft full goats' cheese
Lillet	Semi-sweet wine and brandy aperitif
Limaçon	Name for snail
Limande	Lemon sole or dab
Limat	Name for small snail
Limon	Lime
Limonade	Lemonade
Limousine, à la	Usually with red cabbage and chestnut
Lingue	Ling fish
Liqueur	Liqueur
Liquoreux	Term for very sweet wine
Liquoreux, liquoreuse	Very sweet
Lirac, AC	Red and rosé from Southern Rhone
Listrac, AC	Full reds from Bordeaux commune
Lit	Bed
Littorine	A name for winkle
Livarot	Cylindrical soft, strong cows' cheese often grass-wrapped
Livèche	Lovage
Livron	Strong goats' cheese
Local	Local
Loche	Loach fish
Loire	Major wine area of Northwestern and central France

Lompe	Lumpfish
Long, longue	Long
Longe	Loin
Longeole	Type of sausage
Longuet	Small breadstick
Loquette	Tusk or cusk fish
Lorette, pommes de terre	Crescent-shape of cheesy puréed potato
Lorgnette	Long thin rolled fish fillet
Lormes	Small firm goats' cheese
Lorraine	Northeastern region with light red, rosé and white wines
Lotte	Monkfish
Lotte de rivière, de lac	Burbot fish, freshwater
Lou	Place: usually means a house speciality in Provence
Lou cagarolat	Snail
Loubine	Sea bass, also name for grey mullet
Loudes	Firm round blue cows' cheese
Louise-bonne	Pear
Loukenka	Small spicy sausage
Loup	Sea bass
Loup marin	Wolf-fish or catfish
Loupiac, AC	Sweet white from Bordeaux
Lourmarine	Type of almond
Loutrip	Black pudding
Louvine	Sea bass
Lucas, hareng	Smoked herrings fillets with dill and mustard mayonnaise
Ludon	Commune in Haut-Medoc, Bordeaux
Luizet	Type of apricot

Luma	A small snail
Lusignan	Soft creamy goats' cheese
Lussac-St-Émilion, AC	Full Bordeaux red from near St Emilion
Lyonnais	Usually with onions and cream

Macaire, pommes de terre	Fried cakes of mashed potato
Macaron	Macaroon
Macaroni	Macaroni
Macédoine	Diced mixed vegetables or fruits
Macéré	Macerated
Mâche	Lamb's lettuce
Mâché	Sick wine (mashed)
Macis	Mace
Mâcon Supérieur, AC	Mostly whites and some reds, higher in alcohol than ordinary Macon
Mâcon, AC	Good Burgundy whites, some red from Mâconnais district
Mâcon-Blanc-Villages, AC	Good white, usually from more than one of the forty-three Macon communes
Mâcon-Charnay, AC	Good white from individual Macon commune
Mâcon-Clessé, AC	Good white from individual Macon commune
Mâcon-Fuissé, AC	Good white from individual Macon commune
Mâcon-Lugny, AC	Good Burgundy white from individual Macon commune

Mâcon-Prissé, AC	Good white from individual Macon commune
Mâcon-Uchizy, AC	Good white from individual Macon commune
Mâcon-Viré, AC	Good white from individual Macon commune
Mâconnais	Small conical goats' cheese
Mâconnaise, à la	Usually with wine, onions and mushrooms
Macre	Water chestnut
Macreuse	Wild duck
Macreuse	Shoulder of beef
Madeleine	Small shell-shaped spongecake
Madère	Madeira
Maderisé	Maderised: wine that has been oxidised
Madiran, AC	Deep purple wine from Southwest
Madrilène	Usually with tomatoes
Magistère	Meat and vegetable soups
Magnum	Double bottle (1.5 litres)
Magnum	Rich very creamy cows' cheese
Magravan	Wine with added spirit, and sugar
Magret	Breast of duck
Maigre	Thin, lean
Maigre	Meagre fish, similar to sea bass
Maigret	Breast of duck
Maingaux	Whipped cream and sour cream mixed
Mainotte	Type of mushroom
Maïs	Maize, corn

Maïs, flocons de	Cornflakes
Maison	House or business house
Maison, spécialité de la	House-special
Maître d'hotel	Headwaiter
Maître d'hotel, beurre	Parsley butter
Maître de chai	Cellar master
Majouran	Orange wine liqueur
Malbec	Red wine grape, especially in Bordeaux
Mâle	Male of species: eg cock, buck
Malette	Name for red mullet
Malouine	St Malo-style: often with herb mayonnaise and chopped eggs
Maltaise	Usually with oranges, or blood oranges
Malvoisie, vin de	Malmsey wine from Madeira
Mamirolle	Red coated cows' cheese
Manchon	Small almond cake
Mandarine	Mandarin orange liqueur
Mandarine	Mandarin orange
Mandoline	Implement for slicing vegetables
Mange-tout	Sugar pea, or snow pea
Mangue	Mango
Manière, à la	In the style of
Manouls	Lambs' tripe dish
Manque	A Parisian sponge cake
Maquereau	Mackerel
Maquereau espagnol	Chub mackerel
Maraîchère, à la	Usually with a variety of vegetables

Marais	Market garden
Marasme	Mushroom
Marasquin	Maraschino cherry
Marbrade	Jellied pig's head
Marbré	Striped bream
Marc	Spirit distilled from residue of grapes after pressing
Marc	White spirit made from residue of grapes after juice extracted
Marc	Residue of grapes
Marcassin	Young boar
Marcellin	Almond pastry
Marchand de vin	Wine-merchant
Marchand de Vin, sauce	Red wine, onion and meat sauce
Maréchale, à la	Usually dipped in egg and breadcrumbs, then fried
Marée	Seafood
Marenne	Cultivated oyster
Marette	Bread, especially for bouillabaisse
Margaux, AC	Very good Bordeaux red wine
Marieta	A small flat lobster
Marignan	Small liqueur-soaked Parisian cake
Marin	Sailor
Marinade	Marinating liquid
Mariné, marinée	Marinated
Marinière, à la	Usually shellfish cooked with wine and shallots
Marinoun	Large pork sausage
Marjolaine	Marjoram
Marlamat	Armed gurnard

Marmande	A large flat tomato
Marmelade	Thick sweet fruit purée
Marmite	A tall stew pot
Marmotte	Type of cherry
Marocaine	Usually with courgettes and peppers
Maroilles	Strong soft square cows' cheese
Marouette	Marsh bird, similar to quail
Marque	Brand
Marque, grande	Denotes one of the sixteen leading champagne houses
Marquis	Rich chocolate sponge cake or dessert
Marquise	Very sweet pear
Marquisette	Small chocolate cake
Marron	Chestnut
Marron glacé	Crystallised chestnut
Marsanne	Grape
Marseillaise	Often with garlic, olives and anchovies
Martin-sec	Pear
Mas	Southern French term for vineyard
Mascotte	A coffee cake
Masillon	Small almond tart
Massepain	Marzipan
Matafan	Large pancake
Matelote	Stew, usually of freshwater fish
Matignon	Vegetables sautéed in butter
Maury rancio	Aged sweet wine with tangy taste
Maury, VDN	Sweet red, or rosé from Roussillon

Mauve	Mallow plant
Mayette	Type of walnut
Mayonnaise	Cold sauce of eggyolk and oil
Mazagran	Potato tart
Mazarin	Sponge cake with sugared fruits
Médaillon	Thin round slice, especially of beef
Médoc noir	Merlot grape
Médoc, AC	Wine area of Bordeaux with good to very good reds
Meilleraye de Bretagne	Light yellow square cows' cheese
Mejanels	Vermicelli used in soup
Mélange	Mixture
Mélasse	Treacle
Melba, pêche	Peach ice-cream with raspberry sauce
Melba, toast	Thin toast
Mélé-cass	Marc and blackcurrant liqueur
Melet	Small sandsmelt
Meli-melo	Jumble or mixture
Mélisse	Lemon balm
Melon	Melon
Melon sucrin	Honeydew melon
Melongène	Aubergine
Melsat	White pudding sausage
Melva	Type of small tuna
Menagère, à la	Home-style: usually with vegetables
Mendole commune	Sea bream
Menetou-salon, AC	Good whites, some red from Loire
Menon	Roasted kid

Menouille	Salt pork and beans
Menthe	Mint
Menthe, crème de	Peppermint-flavour liqueur
Menu	The set, fixed price meal
Mer	Sea
Mercurey, AC	Very good Burgundy red wines from the Côte Chalonnaise
Mère	Mother
Mère Poulard	Creator of famous plain omelette
Merguez	Thin spicy sausage
Meringue	Baked egg white and sugar
Merise	Wild cherry
Merlan	Whiting
Merle	Type of wrasse
Merle	Blackbird: used in pâté
Merlot	Red grape variety, especially Bordeaux
Merlu	Hake
Merluche	Another name for hake
Merluche noire	A name for coalfish
Merluchon	Small hake
Mérou	Grouper
Mesclou	Plum and walnut liqueur
Mesclun	Mixed green salad leaves
Mesnil-sur-oger, le	Superior champagne vineyard
Messire-jean	Type of pear
Méthode champenoise	Method whereby champagne gets its sparkle in bottle, not cask
Methuselah	Bottle holding eight bottles
Mets	Dish or course

Metton	Strong, lumpy, cooked cows' cheese
Meture	Corn fritter with ham and eggs
Meuille	Another name for mullet
Meunier	Type of grape variety
Meunière, à la	Usually floured, cooked in butter
Meurette	Usually red wine, bacon and onion sauce
Meursault, AC	Very good Burgundy white wine from Côte de Beaune
Mi-chèvre	Cheese of goats' milk mixed with cows' milk
Miche	Large round loaf
Michon	Apple pancake
Midi	Large Southern French wine-growing area
Midi	Midday
Mie	Soft, crustless bread
Mie, pain de	Sliced, packaged white bread
Miel	Honey
Miel de lavandre	Lavender honey
Miel de toutes fleures	Honey from various flowers
Mietle	A crumb or morsel
Mignardise	Small sweetmeat, petit-four
Mignon	Small, dainty
Mignot	Tangy firm yellow cows' cheese
Mijot	Soup of red wine with bread
Mijoté, mijotée	Simmered
Mijoter	To simmer
Milanaise, à la	Usually with egg, breadcrumbs and cheese
Milandre	A small shark

Millas	Cake of solid maize flour porridge, usually fried, and served cold
Millat	Batter cake of maize flour porridge, often fruit topped
Mille-feuille	Thin layers of puff pastry
Milles	Maize flour pastry
Millésime	Term for vintage
Millet	Millet
Millias	Small maize flour cake
Mimolette	Large firm orange-coated cows' cheese
Mimosa	Usually with chopped hard-boiled egg yolk; also a buck's fizz
Minard	A name for octopus
Minceur	Slimness
Minceur, cuisine	Slim cuisine
Minéral, minérale	Mineral
Minérale, eau	Mineral water
Minervoise, AC	Red, white and rosé from Midi
Minute	Quickly fried with butter
Minute, à la	Cooked to order
Mique	Maize flour dumplings
Mirabeau, à la	Usually with anchovy, olives and tarragon
Mirabelle	Small yellow plum
Mireille, sauce	Hollandaise with tomato purée and basil
Mirepoix	Diced carrots, celery and onions
Mireval	Sweet white wine from Hérault
Mirliton	Pastry tart usually with almond filling

Miroir	Mirror, or glossy film over dish, especially baked eggs
Mis	Placed
Mis en bouteilles	Bottled
Missoun	Provençal peasant sausage
Miton	Middle-cut of salmon
Mode, à la	In the manner of
Moelle	Bone marrow
Moelleux	Term for very sweet white wine
Moelleux, moelleuse	Soft, mellow, velvety
Mogette	Haricot bean
Moitié	Half
Moka	Coffee-flavoured
Mokatine	Tiny coffee-flavoured cake
Mol, molle	Soft
Mollet, mollette	Softish
Mollets, ouefs	Soft-boiled eggs
Monbazillac, AC	Sweet white wine from Perigord
Mondeuse	Red wine grape variety wine
Monegasque	Monaco-style, often with tuna, tomatoes and olives
Mongetado	Haricot bean and pork stew
Monopole	Whole vineyard area belongs to one owner
Monsieur-fromage	Speckled red and white coated cows' cheese
Mont Cenis	Strong blue cows' and goats' cheese
Mont d'or	Small, round blue-rind cows' or goats' cheese from Lyon
Mont des cats	Pressed uncooked cows' cheese

Mont-blanc	Cream-topped chestnut dessert
Montagnarde, soupe	Thick vegetable soup with grated cheese topping
Montagne	Mountain
Montagne-St.Émilion, AC	Good Bordeaux reds
Montagny, AC	Good white Burgundy from Côte Châlonnaise
Montgolfier	Fish stuffed with truffles, lobster and mushroom
Monthélie, AC	Good to very good Burgundy reds, some white, a little sparkling
Montlouis, AC	Sweetish white Loire whites
Montmorency	Type of cherry
Montoire	Conical goats' cheese
Montrachet	Soft creamy goats' cheese
Montrachet, AC	Very good Burgundy white wine from Côte de Beaune
Montravel, AC	Dry, medium sweet Bergerac white
Montsegur	Black-coated round cows' cheese
Moque	Spicy bun
Morbier	Strong firm round cows' cheese, with black streaky coating
Morceau	Small piece, a little bit
Morey-Saint-Denis, AC	Full Burgundy reds, some white
Morgon, AC	Red wine from one of the ten leading Beaujolais villages
Morille	Morel mushroom
Morillon	Variety of black grape
Mornay	White sauce with cheese

Mortadelle	Mortadella sausage
Morue	Salt cod
Mosaïque	A pattern of ingredients
Mostelle	Small seafish, similar to ling, also forkbeard fish
Motelle	Rockling
Mothay	Strong tasting goats' cheese
Mothe-bougon	Small round goats' cheese
Mou	Flat (as wine); also soft
Mou	Animal lungs or lights
Mouclade	Dish of mussels in cream sauce with saffron
Mouflon	Wild sheep
Mougette	Type of haricot bean
Moule	Mussel
Moule barbue	Horse mussel
Moulé, moulée	Moulded
Moules, à la marinière	Mussels with white wine, shallots and parsley
Moulin	Mill
Moulin à poivre	Pepper mill
Moulin-à-Vent, AC	Red wine from one of the ten top Beaujolais villages
Moulis, AC	Good reds from Medoc in Bordeaux
Moulu, moulue	Ground
Mourgeto	Small snail
Mourre agut	Sea bream
Mourvedre	Red wine grape, mainly Midi
Mousquetaire, sauce	Mayonnaise with meat-glaze and shallots
Mousse	Bubbles (as in champagne)
Mousse	Cold frothy mixture

Mousseline	Very light frothy mixture, often with added cream
Mousseron	Type of mushroom
Mousseux	Term for sparkling wine
Mousseux, mousseuse	Frothy
Moustille	Semi-sparkling; just a trace of effervescence
Mout	Must (of wine)
Moutarde	Mustard
Moutardelle	Type of horseradish
Mouton	Sheep, mutton
Muge	A name for grey mullet
Mulard	Type of duck
Mulet	Grey mullet
Mulet doré	Golden grey mullet
Mulet lippu	Thick-lipped mullet
Mulet porc	Thin-lipped grey mullet
Mulet sauteur	Leaping grey mullet
Munster	Soft round golden tangy cows' cheese
Munster au cumin	Munster cheese with cumin or caraway
Mûre	Mulberry
Mûre sauvage	Blackberry
Murene	Moray eel
Murol	Mild, firm round cows' cheese
Murçon	Type of sausage
Mûron	A name for blackberry
Muscade	Nutmeg
Muscadelle	Variety of sweet wine grape
Muscadelle	Type of pear
Muscadet	White wine grape

Muscadet de Sèvre-et-Maine	A generally superior Muscadet from south-east of Nantes
Muscadet, AC	Dry white Loire wine
Muscadet sur lie	Muscadet left lying on its lees or sediment
Muscat	Sweet white wine, sweet musky table and wine grape
Muscat de Beaume de Venise, VDN	Sweet white dessert wine from Rhône valley village
Muscat de Frontignan, VDN	Sweet white from Midi
Muscat de Lunel, VDN	Sweet white from Midi
Muscat de Rivesaltes	Sweet white from Midi
Musclé	Name for a mussel
Muscovite	Moscow-style: usually a cold or frosted desert
Museau	Muzzle, especially of ox, served brawn style
Musette, en	Meat, boned and rolled into ball shape
Muté	Fortified with alcohol
Mye	Clam
Myrte	Myrtle
Myrtille	Bilberry
Mystère	Usually dish of ice-cream and meringue

Nage, à la	Crustaceans cooked by poaching in a herb and wine stock
Nageoire	Fin
Nageur	Small crab
Nantais	Term for a duckling
Nantais	Strong, square cows' cheese
Nantua, à la	Usually with crayfish tails
Napolitaine, tranche	Slice of different flavours of ice-cream and iced mousse
Nappage	Coating (of sauce)
Nappe	Table cloth
Natte	Plaited bread loaf
Nature	Plain; unsweetened
Navarin	Stew of lamb or mutton
Navet	Turnip
Néac, AC	Bordeaux red, now combined with Lalande-de Pomerol appellation
Nectarine	Nectarine
Nèfle	Tart, wine-flavoured fruit
Négociant	Wine bottler and or shipper
Négociant-éleveur	Wine dealer who ages and bottles wines
Nègre	Type of mushroom
Negresse	Name for black potato
Neige	Snow

Neige, oeufs à la	Poached egg whites on custard
Nêne	Aniseed cake
Néroli	Orange blossom oil
Nesselrode	Ice-cream with chestnut purée
Neufchâtel	Small soft white cows' cheese
Nez fleuri	Flowery nose (as wine)
Niçoise	Nice style usually with tomato, garlic, olives, anchovy and basil
Nid	Nest, especially of potatoes
Nielle	Allspice
Nigelle	Black cumin spice
Niolo	Tangy goats' or sheep's cheese
Nivernaise, à la	Usually with carrots, onions
Noël	Christmas
Noilly Prat	A fine vermouth
Noir, noire	Black
Noisette	Hazelnut
Noisettine	Hazelnut pastry
Noix	Nut; especially walnut
Noix d'acajou	Cashew nut
Noix de coco	Coconut
Noix du Bresil	Brazil nut
Noix vertes	A name for pistachio nuts
Nominoë	Creamy chestnut soup
Nonnat	Very tiny fish, often fried
Nonnette	Small gingerbread cake
Nonpareil	Variety of caper
Nonpareil	Variety of pear
Noque	Small creamy dumpling
Norberte	Plum jam

Nord	North
Norelle	Small cider-soaked cake
Normande, à la	Usually with cream, cider, calvados or apples
Norvegiènne, omelette	Spongecake, ice-cream, meringue dessert, served hot
Note	Term for the bill
Nougat	Soft, nutty sweet
Nougatine	Chocolate-iced nutty sponge
Nouilles	Long noodles
Nouillettes	Small noodles
Nouret	Type of mushroom
Nouveau, nouvelle	New
Nouvelle cuisine	New, lighter style of cooking
Nouzillards au lait	Milky chestnut soup
Noyau	Kernel
Nuits-St-Georges, AC	Good red Burgundy wine from the Côtes de Nuits
Nulle	Musk-flavoured egg custard
Nuque	Maize fritter

Oblade	Type of sea bream
Occitane, à l'	Usually with tomatoes and garlic
Oeillade	A table grape
Oeillet	Carnation: used for syrup and liqueur
Oeuf	Egg
Oeuf de Pâques	Easter egg
Oeuf du jour	Fresh-laid egg
Oeuf, blanc d'	Egg white
Oeuf, jaune d'	Egg yolk
Oeufs à la coque	Soft-boiled, served in the shell
Oeufs au miroir	Fried eggs
Oeufs à la poêle	Fried eggs
Oeufs brouillés	Scrambled eggs
Oeufs dubois	Scrambled eggs with lobster
Oeufs dur	Hard-boiled eggs
Oeufs en cocotte	Eggs baked in an individual dish
Oeufs frits	Fried eggs
Oeufs mollets	Soft-boiled, served out of shell
Oeufs pochés	Poached eggs
Oeufs sur le plat	Fried eggs
Oie	Goose
Oignon	Onion
Oignonade	Onion stew

Oiseau	Bird
Oison	Gosling
Oleron	Creamy fresh ewes' cheese
Olive	Olive
Olive de mer	Wedge-shell clam
Olives cassés	Cracked olives in fennel and salt water
Olivet	Small cows' cheese, often leaf-wrapped
Olivet bleu	Small round cows' cheese often leaf-wrapped, some blue mould
Olivet cendré	Small cows' cheese, ash-coated, often leaf-wrapped
Olivette	A name for a scallop
Olivette blanche	Type of white table grape
Omble chevalier	Char fish, similar to salmon
Ombrine	Umbrine, similar to sea bass
Omelette	Omelette
Onglet	Flank, usually of beef
Opera	Fat long white bread loaf
Or	Gold
Orange	Orange
Orange givré	Orange filled with sorbet
Orangeat	Candied orange peel
Ordinaire	Common
Ordinaire, vin	Ordinary, everyday wine
Oreille	Ear, usually of pig or calf
Oreille de mer	Abalone
Oreillette	Very small pig's ear
Oreillon	Small ear, or ear-shape
Orge	Barley
Oriental(e)	Oriental, often with rice and saffron

Origan	Oregano
Orléanaise, à la	Often with chicory, potatoes
Ormeau	Abalone
Ormier	Abalone
Oronge	Type of mushroom
Orphie	Garfish
Ortie	Nettle
Ortie de mer	Sea anemone
Ortolan	Small game bird, fattened up before eating
Os	Bone
Osciètre	Type of sturgeon and its caviar
Oseille	Sorrel
Ossau	Firm strong ewes' cheese
Oublie	Thin wafer
Ouest	West
Ouillade	Thick soup of cabbage and bean
Oursin	Sea-urchin
Oursinade, oursinado	Soup of sea urchins
Outarde	Bustard
Ouvert, ouverte	Open
Ouvre-boîte	Tin-opener
Oyonade	Rich goose stew

Pacaret	With added sherry
Pachade	Prune omelette
Pacherenc du Vic-Bilh, AC	Sweet whites from Pyrenées
Pageot rouge	Pandora bream
Pagre	Variety of seabream
Pagre royal	Type of bream
Paillarde	Thin flat grilled slice, especially of veal
Paille	Straw: used to dry grapes in making sweet wine of Jura
Paille, pommes de terre	Very thin potato chips
Paillette d'oignon	Deep-fried onion rings
Paillette dorée	Cheese straw
Pain	Bread
Pain au levain	Yeast bread
Pain bis	Brown bread
Pain brioche	Brioche loaf
Pain complet	Wholemeal bread
Pain d'antan	Wheat and rye bread
Pain d'épices	Gingerbread
Pain de campagne	Large round peasant loaf
Pain de gênes	Genoa sponge cake
Pain de mie	Sliced, packaged white bread
Pain de seigle	Rye bread
Pain de son	Bran bread

Pain entier	Wholemeal bread
Pain grillé	Toast
Pain perdu	French toast
Pain rassis	Stale bread
Pain suédois	Crispbread
Pain, gros	Large crusty loaf
Pain, petit	Bread roll
Paladru	Cows' cheese from Savoy
Palaille	Very small sardines
Palais de boeuf	Ox palate
Palangre	Type of fishing line
Palefour	Bacon tart
Paleron	Shoulder of beef
Palet	Minced beef patty
Palet de dames	Small thin iced biscuit
Palette	Blade bone
Palette, AC	Provence red and rosé wines
Pallason	Flat potato cake
Palmier	Small heart-shaped pastry
Palombe	Wild pigeon
Palomet	Type of mushroom
Palomète	Type of tuna fish
Palomine	Pompano fish
Palourde	Clam
Palourdes farcies	Clams, stuffed with shallots, grilled with cheese
Pamplemousse	Grapefruit
Pan bagna	Bread with olive oil, garlic, olives, anchovies, peppers and onion
Panache	Shandy
Panaché, panachée	Mixed
Panade	Soup of bread, milk and eggs
Panais	Parsnip

Pané	Breadcrumbed
Panier	Basket
Panisse	Fried cake of chick peas
Pannequet	Sweet or savoury pancake
Pannes cendré	Strong ash-coated cows' cheese
Panoufle	Part of beef sirloin
Pantin	Small pork-filled patty
Panure	Breadcrumbs
Papayer	Papaya or pawpaw
Papeton	Corn cob
Papier d'aluminium	Tinfoil
Papier sulfurisé	Greaseproof paper
Papillotte	Paper or foil pouch
Papillotte, en	Food cooked in paper, foil pouch or envelope
Paprika	Paprika
Pâquerette	Daisy: leaves eaten in salad
Pâques	Easter
Paquette	Female lobster with eggs
Parc	Oyster bed
Parfait	Iced mousse
Parfait-amour	Sweet-scented violet liqueur
Parfum	Flavour
Paris-brest	Choux pastry with almonds
Parme	Amberjack fish
Parmentier	With potatoes
Parmentier, hachis	Shepherd's pie
Parmentier, potage	Potato and leek soup
Parmesane, à la	With parmesan cheese
Partager	To share
Pascade	Type of pancake
Pascado	Bacon omelette
Passarelle	Dried muscat grapes

Passé, passée	Strained
Passe-crassane	Type of pear
Passe-l'an	Large round hard cows' cheese
Passe-pierres	Type of seaweed, often pickled
Passe-tout-grains, AC	Light Burgundy reds and some rosé
Pastègue	Sea anemone
Pasteque	Watermelon
Pastille	Small sweet
Pastis	Liquorice-flavoured aperitif
Pastissoun	Orange-flavoured pastry
Pastourelle, à la	Shepherd's style
Patacle	A name for sea bream
Patate	Common term for potato
Patate	Sweet potato
Pâté	Meat and fat mixture, usually pork, baked in terrine, eaten cold
Pâte	Pastry, dough; pasta; paste
Pâté	Pie or dish with pastry crust
Pâte, petit	Pasty or patty
Pâté chou	Chou pastry
Pâte à frire	Batter
Pâté brise	Short pastry
Pâté d'amandes	Almond paste
Pâté de campagne	Usually rough terrine of pork, herbs
Pâté de Chatres	Partridge paté
Pâté de guimauve	Marshmallow
Pâté feuilletée	Puff pastry
Pâté maison	Usually smooth terrine with liver made on premises

Pâté sablée	Sweet pastry
Pâté vendéen	Rabbit paté
Patelle	Limpet or barnacle
Patisserie	Pastry shop or pastries
Patisson	Squash, marrow
Patron	Proprietor
Patte	Paw
Pauillac, AC	Good to very good Bordeaux red from Haut-Medoc
Paupiette, en	Stuffed, rolled then braised slice of meat or fish
Pavé	Small square sponge cake
Pavé d'auge	Square soft spicy cows' cheese
Pavé de moyaux	Square soft spicy cows' cheese
Pavé	General term for a yellow-coated square cows' cheese
Pavé	Square moulded dish
Pavé	A thick steak
Pavie	Type of peach
Pavot	Poppy
Pavot, grains de	Poppy seeds
Payer	To pay
Pays	Country or region
Paysanne, à la	Peasant-style
Peau, peaux	Skin
Pec, hareng	Fresh salted herring
Pécharmant, AC	Full reds from Bergerac
Pêche	Peach
Pêche abricotée	Yellow peach
Pêche blanche	White peach
Pêche jaune	Yellow peach

Péché	Naughty (but nice)
Pêcheur	Fisherman
Peigne glabre	Type of scallop
Pelamide	Bonito fish
Pélardon d'Altier	Small soft goats' cheese
Pélardon de ruoms	Small, soft, nutty goats' cheese
Pêlardon des Cévennes	Small round soft goats' cheese
Pélerine	A name for a scallop
Pélou	A name for a small crab
Pelures	Usable vegetable trimmings, especially of truffles and mushrooms
Peral	Sheep's cheese on straw
Perche	Perch, the freshwater fish
Perche de mer	A name for sea bass
Perchette	Young perch
Perdreau	Young partridge
Perdrix	Partridge
Père tranquil, potage du	Soup of puréed lettuce
Perlant	Slightly sparkling
Perlé	Slightly sparkling (wine)
Perle	Pearl
Perles du Japon	Tapioca
Perlot	A small oyster
Pernand-Vergelesses, AC	Good red and white Burgundy wine from Côte de Beaune
Pernod	Brand of anisette aperitif
Persil	Parsley
Persillade	Chopped parsley, garlic and shallots

Persillé	Blue-veined, as cheese
Persillé	Marbled (as meat)
Persillé de thones	Tangy blue goats' cheese
Persillé des aravis	Tangy blue goats' cheese
Persillé	Garnished with parsley
Pessac	Commune in Graves appellation with some superior reds and whites
Pet de nonne	Light fluffy fritter
Peteran	Stew of sheep's tripe and ham
Pétillant	With a slight fizz or sparkle
Petit beurre	Small biscuit
Petit déjeuner	Breakfast
Petit four	Small sweet biscuit
Petit gris	Type of mushroom
Petit gris	Small snail
Petit lait	Whey
Petit Lisieux	Small round strong cows' cheese
Petit Marcellin	Small almond pastry
Petit pain	Bread roll
Petit pied bleu	Type of mushroom
Petit pois	Young green peas
Petit pot de creme	Rich creamy egg custard dessert
Petit poussin	Very small spring chicken
Petit salé	Salt pork
Petit, petite	Small
Petit-chablis	Less expensive white Burgundy from Chablis area
Petit-houx	Broom plant
Petit-suisse	Fresh, unsalted soft cows' cheese

Petit-verdot	red wine grape variety, especially of Bordeaux
Petite marmite	Small pot of meat broth
Petits ventres	Stuffed mutton belly
Petits-châteaux	Usually good value reds from lesser known Bordeaux producers
Pétoncle	Small queen scallop
Pholiote	Type of mushroom
Pibales	Small fried eels
Pic	Woodpecker
Pic-poul	White wine grape variety, especially southern France
Picadou	Strong vine-wrapped cheese, aged in wine
Picarel	Sea bream
Picaut	Turkey
Piccardan	Red wine grape, especially used in Château-Neuf-du-Pape
Picherel	Anisette liqueur
Pichet	Jug, pitcher
Picholine	Type of large olive
Picodon de dieulefit	Small round tangy goats' cheese
Picodon de l'Ardèche	Small soft mellow goats' cheese
Picodon de St Agrève	Small round goats' cheese
Picodon de Valréas	Soft round nutty goats' cheese
Picon	Orange-flavoured aperitif
Picoler	To tipple, to drink a lot
Picpoul	Type of white wine grape
Picrate	Plonk
Pièce de boeuf	Rump of beef

Pied	Foot
Pied de mouton blanc	Type of mushroom
Pied de porc	Pig's trotter
Pied-de-cheval	Name for type of large oyster
Pieds et paquets	Sheep's tripe and trotters
Pierre-qui-vire	Flat strong cows' cheese with red rind
Pieuvre	Octopus
Pigeon	Pigeon
Pigeonneau	Young pigeon
Pignon	Pine kernel
Pigouille	Small fresh creamy cows'/goats'/ewes' cheese on straw
Pilau	Savoury rice
Pilet	Type of wild duck
Pilon	Drumstick
Pilpil	Name for salt cod with garlic
Piment basquais	Paprika
Piment doux	Sweet pepper
Piment fort rouge	Chilli
Pimentée	Peppery, hot or spicy
Pimpernelle	Burnet, the salad leaf
Pin	Pine tree
Pinard	Plonk
Pince	Claw
Pineau d'Aunis	Red wine grape, especially used in Loire
Pineau des Charentes	Aperitif wine: blend of young wine and cognac
Pinée	Dried cod
Pinot	Type of grape
Pinot blanc	White wine grape, especially Burgundy

Pinot gris	White wine grape
Pinot Liebault	Red wine grape
Pinot Meunier	Red wine grape
Pinot Noir	Red wine grape, especially Burgundy
Pintade	Guinea fowl
Pintadeau	Young guinea fowl
Pipérade	Omelette or scrambled eggs with chopped tomato, peppers and onion
Piquant	Piquant
Piqué	Larded
Pique-nique	Picnic
Piqué	Term for over-acidic wine
Pire	Pork lungs cooked in wine with blood
Pirot	Dish of goat with garlic and sorrel
Pissaladière	Open tart topped with onion, olives, anchovies and tomatoes
Pissalat	Puree of oil, anchovies and cloves
Pissenlit	Name for dandelion
Pistache	Pistachio
Pistache, en	A dish garnished with garlic cloves
Pistil	Hot savoury cheese pasty
Pistole	Type of prune
Pistou	Sauce of basil, garlic, oil and often pine kernels
Pithiviers	Almond puff pastry cake
Pithiviers au foin	Hay-coated soft cows' cheese
Pivarunta	Goat and pepper stew
Pivoulade	Type of mushroom

Plaisir	Small wafer biscuit
Planche	Wooden platter
Plat	Dish or plate
Plat du jour	Dish of the day
Plat principal	Main course
Plat, plate	Flat
Plat-de-cotes	Flank
Plate	Type of flat oyster
Plateau	Tray or platter
Pleurote	Type of mushroom
Plie	Plaice
Pluche	Small leaf
Plus	More
Pluvier	Plover bird
Pochade	Stew of freshwater fish
Poché, pochée	Poached
Pocheteau	Type of skate
Pocheteau noir	Long-nosed skate
Poêle	Frying pan; pan
Poêle, oeufs a la	Fried eggs
Poêlé, poêlée	Pot-roasted
Poêlon	Lidded pot
Pogne	Fruit or jam filled brioche
Point, à	Medium-done, as steak
Point, à	Ready for eating, as cheese
Point, à	Ripe, as fruit
Pointe	Tip
Pointe de culotte	Top rump of beef
Poire	Pear
Poire de terre	Jerusalem artichoke
Poire Williams	Pear spirit
Poire williams	Type of pear
Poireau	Leek

Pois	Pea
Pois cassés	Split peas
Pois chiches	Chick peas
Poison	Poison
Poisson	Fish
Poisson pilote	Pilot fish
Poisson volant	Flying fish
Poissonaille	Very young fish, fry
Poissonerie	Fishmonger's shop
Poissonnier	Fishmonger
Poissonière	Fish kettle
Poitrine	Breast
Poivrade, sauce	Peppery brown sauce
Poivre	Pepper
Poivre blanc	White pepper
Poivre d'Âne	Soft herby round goats' cheese
Poivre en grains	Peppercorns
Poivre noir	Black pepper
Poivré	Peppered
Poivron	Red or green sweet pepper
Polente	Thick porridge of maize meal usually sliced and fried
Polonnais	Usually with chopped egg and parsley
Pomerol, AC	Good, some very good Bordeaux reds
Pommard, AC	Good red Burgundy wine from Côte de Beaune
Pomme	Apple
Pomme de terre	Potato
Pommes de terre en l'air	Potato puffs
Pommes de terre au four	Baked jacket potato

Pommes en l'air	Fried apple slices
Pommes frites	Potato chips
Pommes pont neuf	Párisian term for potato chips
Pompe	Pastry with fried pork cubes
Pompe aux grattons	Pork and pork crackling in pastry
Pomponette	Savoury pastry
Pont-l'Évêque	Square yellow-coated cows' cheese
Pont neuf	Almond puff pastry
Pontgibaud	Aged blue cows' cheese
Porc	Pork
Porc, fromage de	Brawn
Porcelet	Suckling pig
Porché	Stewed pigs' trotters and ears
Porchetta	Whole suckling pig, spit-roasted
Pormonier	Herby sausage
Port-Salut	Round, firm but soft pressed cows' cheese
Porto	Port wine
Portugaise	Portuguese oyster
Pot	Pot, jar
Pot	Small bottle or carafe: 50 cl
Pot-au-crême	Rich cream custard
Pot-au-feu	Boiled meat and vegetables cooked in the same pot
Potable	Drinkable, especially of water
Potable, eau	Drinking water
Potage	Thickened soup
Potée	Very thick soup of meat, potatoes and vegetables
Potiquet	Small earthenware dish
Potiron	Large pumpkin
Pouce-pied	Goose-necked barnacle

Pouding	Plum pudding
Poudre	Powder
Poudre, en	Ground
Pouillard	Young partridge
Pouilly-Fuissé, AC	Good Burgundy white from the Mâçonnais region
Pouilly-Fumé, AC	Dry whites from Loire
Pouilly-Loché, AC	Full white Burgundy from Maçonnais region
Pouilly-sur-Loire, AC	Dry white Loire
Pouilly-Vinzelles, AC	Good Burgundy white from Maçonnais region
Poularde	Roasting chicken
Poule	Boiling hen
Poule au pot	Chicken, stuffed and cooked in pot with vegetables
Poule-au-pot	Chicken and beef stew
Poule des bois	Type of grouse
Poulet	Young chicken
Poulet de Bresse	Maize-fed chicken from Bresse
Poulet fermier	Free-range chicken
Poulet jaune	Maize-fed, free-range chicken
Poulette	Pullet, very young chicken
Pouligny-St-Pierre	Tangy soft pyramid goats' cheese
Pouliot	Type of wild mint
Pouloud	Buckwheat dumplings
Poulpe	Octopus
Poulsard	Red-wine grape, especially in Jura
Pountari	Cabbage leaves stuffed with bacon or sausage meat
Poupart	Type of large crab

Poupeton	Small meat roll; also, fish pâté with cheese
Poupre	Octopus
Poupre	Purple
Poupresse	Small octopus
Pouprihoun	Baby octopus
Pourboire	Tip
Pourly	Soft nutty goats' cheese
Pourpier	Salad leaf
Pourri	Rotten
Pourriture noble	'Noble rot' on grapes essential for dessert wines
Pousse-café	Spirit chaser after coffee
Pousse-rapière	Sparkling wine with Armagnac
Poussin	Spring chicken
Poutarge	Dried mullet roe
Poutassou	Blue whiting
Poutine	Minute sardines and anchovies
Poutine nue	Scaleless baby sardines
Praire	Small venus clam
Praline	Mixture of ground nuts, especially caramelised almonds
Praslin	Almond coated in caramel
Pratelle	Type of mushroom
Pré, prés	Meadow
Pré-salé	Salt-marsh
Premier cru	Second highest ranking for AC wines, especially in Bordeaux
Premières Côtes de Blaye, AC	Bordeaux whites, some reds
Prepon	Melon

Pressé	In a hurry
Pressé, citron	Freshly-squeezed lemon juice
Pressé, pressée	Pressed
Pression	Pressure
Pression, bière	Draught beer
Pressoir à vin	Wine press
Presure	Rennet
Prêt	Ready
Prêtre	Sand-smelt
Prévat	Type of mushroom
Primeur	First
Primeur	New wine
Princesse, à la	Usually with truffles, asparagus and cream sauce
Printanière, à la	Usually with spring vegetables
Printemps	Spring
Prix	Price
Prix fixe	Fixed price
Prix de détail	Retail price
Prix de gros	Wholesale price
Profiterole	Small choux pastry
Proposer	To suggest
Propriétaire	Vineyard owner
Propriétaire	Proprietor
Propriétaire-recoltant	Vineyard owner and operator
Propriété	Property, especially vineyard
Protestation	Complaint
Provençale, à la	Usually with garlic, tomatos, onions often olives, anchovies
Provence	Southern French region with rosés, reds and whites
Prune	Plum brandy

Prune	Plum
Pruneau	Prune
Pruneaux fourrés	Stuffed sweet prunes
Prunelle	Wild plum liqueur
Prunelle	Sloe
Prunier	Plum tree
Psalliote	Type of mushroom
Puant	Term for very pungent ('stinking') brine-cured cows' cheese
Puant macéré	Very strong pickled cheese
Puant, puante	Smelly
Puce	Name for a tiny crayfish
Pudding	Steamed pudding
Puisseguin-St-Emilion, AC	Bordeaux reds from Northeastern St Emilion
Puits d'amour	Small filled sweet pastry
Puligny-montrachet, AC	Superior Burgundy whites from Côte de Beaune
Purée	Purée
Purée de pommes de terre	Mashed potato
Pyramide	Pyramid-shaped soft goats' cheese
Pyrenéés-orientales, VDP	Reds and whites from Roussillon

Qualité extra	Top grade of meat at butchers
Quart	Quarter
Quart de vin	Quarter bottle of wine
Quartanier	Four-year-old wild boar
Quartier	Quarter or segment
Quarts-de-chaume, AC	Sweet white wine from Loire
Quasi	Chump end of meat, especially veal
Quatre mendiants	Mixture of hazelnuts, raisins, figs and almonds
Quatre-épices	Mixture of cloves, ginger, whitepepper and nutmeg
Quatre-quarts	Pound cake
Quenelle	Small creamy dumpling
Quetsch	Type of plum
Queue	Tail
Queue de boeuf	Oxtail
Quiche	Savoury egg custard tart
Quichet	Toasted bread with oil and anchovies
Quignon	Large wedge of bread
Quimperlaise	Usually with fish and shellfish
Quincy, AC	Dry white from Loire valley
Quinquina	Quinine-flavoured aperitif
Quintal	Type of white cabbage

Rabes	Salted cods' roes
Rabiole	Type of turnip
Rablay	Part of the Côteaux du Layon appellation: mainly sweet white
Rable	Saddle (especially of rabbit, hare)
Rabotte	Apple wrapped in pastry
Racine	Root, root vegetable
Raclette	Dish of potatoes with melted cheese
Radis	Radish
Rafraîchi, rafraîchie	Cool, refreshing
Ragot	Wild boar
Ragoût	Stew of meat or poultry
Raie	Skate
Raie au beurre noire	Skate with black butter
Raie bouclé	Thornback ray
Raie douce	Spotted ray
Raie miroir	Mirror skate
Raifort	Horseradish
Raioles	Ravioli
Raisin	Grape
Raisin de Corinthe	Currant
Raisin de Smyrne	Sultana
Raisin sec	Raisin
Raisiné	Grape jam

Raiteau	Small skate
Raito	Provence red wine sauce
Raiton	Small skate
Ramequin	Small dish, ramekin
Ramequin de Lagnière	Small hard nutty goats' cheese
Ramereau	Young wood pigeon
Ramier	Wood pigeon
Rancio	Fortified sweet wine
Râpé	Term for grated cheese
Râpé, râpée	Grated
Râpée	Potato pancake
Rapure	Very large oyster, usually cooked
Raquette	Type of partridge
Rascasse	Scorpion fish
Rasoir	Razorshell clam
Raspail	Herbal liqueur
Rassis, rassise	Stale, as bread
Rasteau	Basic reds with Côte du Rhône appellation
Rasteau, VDN	Sweet wines from Rhone valley
Rat	Name for star-gazer fish
Ratafia	Macaroon biscuit
Ratafia, VDL	Sweet wine fortified with brandy made from champagne
Ratatouille	Vegetable stew, especially of aubergine, tomatoes, onion, garlic and peppers
Rate	Spleen, especially pig or ox
Raton	Pastry with cream cheese
Rave	A name for turnip

Ravigotte	Cold sauce with capers and gherkin
Raviolis	Ravioli
Rayoles	Vegetable ravioli with walnuts
Rayon de miel	Honeycomb
Rd	Recently disgorged: richer than usual champagne
Reblochon	Soft flat round mild, golden cows' cheese
Reblochonet	Smooth round cows' cheese
Reboucher	To re-cork
Recette	Recipe
Réchauffée	Reheated
Récollet de gérardmer	Large, creamy cows' cheese from Alsace
Récoltant	Wine grower
Récolte	Wine crop, harvest
Reduction	Sauce thickened by boiling
Régal de sang	Fried cake of poultry blood
Régime	Diet
Régime, au	On a diet
Régional	Local
Réglisse	Liquorice
Régnié, AC	Red wine from one of the ten top Beaujolais villages
Reheboam	Large champagne bottle: equivalent of six ordinary bottles
Reims	Major champagne producing city
Reine des glaces	Iceberg lettuce
Reine des reinettes	Type of apple, similar to Cox's Orange Pippin

Reine, à la	Usually with chicken and mushrooms
Reine-claude	Greengage
Reinette grise	Russet apple
Relais	Inn
Relais routiers	Transport café
Religieuse	Cake of filled, coated choux pastry balls
Religieuse	Jam tart
Rémoise	Reims-style: usually with champagne
Rémoulade	Mayonnaise with capers and gherkin
Repas	Meal
Requin	Shark
Requin marteau	Hammerhead shark
Réservation	Reservation
Réserve	Usually indicates age of spirits
Restes	Left-overs
Reuilly, AC	Good light whites from Loire
Reveillon	Very late supper, especially after midnight mass at Xmas
Rhône	The Rhône valley wine area in Southeastern France
Rhône, du	From the Rhône valley
Rhubarbe	Rhubarb
Rhum	Rum
Ribot, lait	Liquid yoghurt
Ricard	Anis aperitif
Riceys, rosé des, AC	Rosé wine from champagne area
Riche	Rich or sweet, especially of champagne
Riche	Rich

Richebourg, AC	Superb red Burgundy from Côte de Nuit area
Richelieu	Large pastry cake with almond and apricot jam
Riesling	Alsace white wine grape
Rigodon	Sweet or savoury egg flan on brioche base
Rigotte de pelussin	Small round nutty goats' cheese
Rigotte de condrieu	Small soft mild goats' cheese
Rillauds	Small pieces of pork cooked in pork fat and herbs
Rillettes	Smooth mixture of pork, pork fat served cold like paté
Rillons	Small pieces of pork cooked in pork fat and herbs
Rincer la dalle	To whet one's whistle
Rippele	Pork chop in red wine
Ris	Sweetbreads, usually of calf or lamb
Risotto	Risotto: rice cooked in stock
Rissole	Savoury fritter
Rissolé, rissolée	Fried or browned
Rivesaltes, AC	Sweet fortified whites from Midi
Rivière	River
Riz	Rice
Riz a l'impératrice	Rice custard with fruit and cream
Riz au lait	Rice pudding
Riz complet	Brown rice
RM	Recoltant manipulant: producer and grower
Robert	Spicy brown onion sauce
Robinet	Tap

Robinet, eau de	Tapwater
Roblot	Type of small mackerel
Rocamadour	Small round sheep's cheese
Rocambole	Type of small onion
Rochelaise	Usually fish with red wine
Rocher	Rock
Rocher épineaux	Small spiny shellfish
Rogeret	Small soft goats' cheese
Rogeret de cévennes	Small round nutty goats' cheese
Rogne	Paste of fish roe, especially mullet
Rognon	Kidney
Rognonnade	Dish cooked with kidneys
Rognures	Pastry trimmings
Roi	King
Rois, galette de	Special cake served on Twelfth Night
Rollot	Soft tangy yellow cows' cheese
Romaine	Roman-style
Romanée-conti, AC	Burgundy's best red: from the Côte de Nuits area
Romanée-saint-vivant, AC	Very superior red Burgundy from Côtes de Nuits area
Romarin	Rosemary
Rombou	Brill
Romorantin	Blue-coated mild goats' cheese
Romsteak	Rumpsteak
Ronce	Blackberry bush
Ronce, mûre de	Blackberry
Rond de gigot	Cut of mutton
Roquefort	Ewes' cheese with blue mould

Roquette	Rocket, the salad leaf
Roquille	Crystallised orange peel
Rosbif	Roast beef
Rosé	Pink wine made from red wine grapes
Rosé, rosée	Pink
Rosette	Large salami sausage
Rosette, AC	Semi-sweet whites from Bergerac
Rossini	Usually with truffles and foie gras
Rossolis	Fruit-flavoured brandy
Rôti	Roasted
Rôtis au four	Oven-roasted
Rouelle	Round slice
Rougail	Type of spicy seasoning
Rouge	Red
Rouge, vin	Red wine
Rougeot	Smoked duck fillet
Rouget	Red mullet
Rouget barbet	Red mullet
Rouget de roche	Red mullet
Rouille	Spicy mayonnaise with garlic and red pepper
Roulade	Stuffed roll or rolled dish
Roulé, roulée	Rolled
Rousse	Russet
Rousseau	Red sea bream
Rousselet	Russet pear
Roussette	Rock salmon
Roussette, grande	Huss
Roussette, petite	Dogfish
Routier	Lorry driver
Routier, relais	Transport café

Roux	Russet
Roux	Lightly browned butter and flour mix for thickening sauce
Rouy	Strong, soft, square cows' cheese
Royale	Usually with cream sauce and truffles
Royan	Type of large sardine
Rubané, rubanée	Ribboned, striped
Ruche	Beehive (shape)
Ruchottes-Chambertin, AC	Superb red Burgundy from Côte de Nuits area
Rude	Rough (as wine)
Ruffec	Small round fruity goats' cheese
Rully, AC	Good red and white burgundy from the Côte Chalonnaise
Russe	Russian-style
Russule	Type of mushroom
Rutabaga	Swede

Sabayon	Dessert of eggs, wine and sugar
Sable	Sand
Sablé	Shortbread
Sables du Golf du Lion, VDP	Provence red, white or rosé
Sablet	Mostly red wines from Rhône valley commune
Sablier	Egg-timer
Sabodet	Thick slices of pork sausage
Sabot	Clog
Sabot, en	Tucked inside another ingredient
Sabre	Sword, used for opening champagne
Sabre	Scabbard fish
Safran	Saffron
Sagou	Sago
Saignant, saignante	Bleeding
Saignant	Rare, as steak
Saigneux	Term for neck of veal or mutton
Saindoux	Lard
Saint Rémy	Strong, spicy square cows' cheese
Saint-Amour, AC	Red wine from one of the ten leading Beaujolais villages

Saint-Aubin, AC	White Burgundy from Côte de Beaune area
Saint-Benoît	Fruity soft small round cows' cheese
Saint-Bris, sauvignon de, AC	White Burgundy from sauvignon grape grown in Chablis area
Saint-Chinian, AC	Red wine from Languedoc region
Saint-Émilion, AC	Rich full reds from Bordeaux
Saint-Estèphe, AC	Good, some very good red wines from Bordeaux
Saint-Florentin	Small round spicy cows' cheese
Saint-Foy	Cylindrical blue cows' cheese
Saint-Foy-Bordeaux, AC	Sweet whites, dry whites, some red from Eastern Bordeaux
Saint-Georges-St-Émilion, AC	Full Bordeaux reds from Northeastern St Emilion
Saint-Honoré, gâteau	Choux pastry with custard
Saint-Hubert	Rich creamy cows' cheese
Saint-Jacques, coquille	Scallop
Saint-Jean-de-Minervois	Sweet white wine from Aude
Saint-Joseph, AC	Good red, some white Rhône wine
Saint-Julien, AC	Good traditional Bordeaux red from Haut-Médoc
Saint-Lambert-Lattay	Sweet whites from the Coteaux du Layon appellation
Saint-Marcellin	Soft, round cows' cheese with grey rind

Saint-Michel	Coffee sponge cake
Saint-Nectaire	Firm round cows' cheese
Saint-Nicolas-de-Bourgeil, AC	Light reds, some rosés from Loire
Saint-Paulin	Firm mild yellow cows' cheese
Saint-Péray mousseux	Sweet and dry Rhône sparkling
Saint-Péray, AC	Sweet and dry whites from Rhône
Saint-Pierre	John Dory fish
Saint-Pourçain, AC	Dry whites, rosé and light red from Loire valley
Saint-Raphaël	Quinine-flavoured aperitif
Saint-Romain, AC	Burgundy reds, some whites in Côte du Beaune area
Saint-Sardos, VDP	Fruity reds and rosés, dry whites from the Southwest
Saint-Saturnin, AC	Full reds, rosés from Midi
Saint-Seurin-de-Cadourne, AC	Part of the Haut-Medoc AC: full fruity reds
Saint-Sylvestre	New Year's Eve
Saint-Varent	Commercially-produced goats' cheese
Saint-Veran, AC	Dry white Burgundy from the Mâconnais region
Sainte-Croix-du-Mont, AC	Sweet golden whites, some dry whites from Bordeaux
Sainte-Maure	Strong soft cylindrical goats' cheese
Saint-Maure Fermier	Soft full goats' cheese, farm-made with straw centre
Sainte-Menehoud, sauce	Very spicy white sauce
Saison	Season

Saissonier	Seasonal
Salade	Salad
Salade composée	Mixed salad
Salade panachée	Mixed salad
Salade verte	Green salad
Saladier	Salad bowl
Salaisson	Salted foods
Salamanzar	Large bottle: equivalent twelve bottles
Salamis	Salami
Salé, petit	Salt pork
Salé, salée	Salted
Salé, pre-	Salt marshes
Salmigondis	Type of meat stew
Salmis	Roasted meat, poultry finished with wine
Salon de thé	Tea shop
Salpicon	Diced meat and vegetables as stuffing or garnish
Salsifis	Salsify, the vegetable
Sampigny-les-Maranges, AC	Good fruity red Burgundy from Côte de Beaune
Sancerre, AC	Good red, white and rosé Loire wine
Sanciau	Thick pancake
Sandre	Type of river pike-perch
Sandwich	Filled French bread or roll
Sang	Blood
Sanglier	Wild boar
Sanguette	Cooked blood
Sanguin	Type of mushroom
Sanguine	Blood orange
Sans sel	Salt-free
Sansiot	Calf's head

Sansonnet	Small mackerel
Santé	Health
Santé, à votre	Cheers
Santenay, AC	Good red, some white Burgundy from Côte de Beaune
Sapin	Fir tree
Sapindor	Fir tree cone liqueur
Sar	Type of sea bream
Sar doré	Banded bream
Sar royale	Large sea bream
Sarbadin	Pork-based sausage in red wine
Sarcelle	Type of wild duck
Sarde	Sardinian-style
Sardine	Sardine
Sargasse	Type of seaweed, eaten as salad leaf
Sarladais	Usually with truffles
Sarments	Vine twigs
Sarque	Type of sea bream
Sarrasin	Buckwheat
Sarrason	Watered buttermilk, usually eaten on potatoes
Sarriette	Savoury the herb
Sartanado	Tiny fish fried in oil
Sarteno	Strong flat goats' or ewes' cheese
Sassenage	Tangy blue goats' and cows' cheese
Sauce	Sauce
Saucisse	Fresh sausage in raw state
Saucisson	Large raw saveloy, poached and eaten hot

Saucisson sec	Prepared dried sausage, ready to eat, as salami
Sauge	Sage
Saumon	Salmon
Saumon blanc	A name for hake
Saumon fumé	Smoked salmon
Saumoneau	Young salmon
Saumonette	Rock salmon
Saumur, AC	Still and sparkling Loire whites, light fruity reds
Saumur-Champigny, AC	Good red Loire wine
Saumure	Brine
Saumuré	Pickled
Saupe	Type of sea bream
Saur	Salted, smoked herring
Saurel	Horse mackerel
Saussignac, Côtes de, AC	Big, full white from Bergerac
Sausson	Paste of anchovies, olive oil, mint and almonds
Sauté, sautée	Tossed or lightly fried
Sauternes, AC	Full rich sweet dessert white from Bordeaux
Sauvage	Wild
Sauvage	Term for a wild duck
Sauvignon blanc	White wine grape, especially grown in Loire and Bordeaux
Savarin	Yeast-cake, usually soaked in rum
Savaron	Strong grey-coated cows' cheese
Savennières, AC	Strong, dry Loire whites
Saveur	Flavour

Savigny-les-Beaune, AC	Good red Burgundy wine from the Côte de Beaune
Savoie	Alpine wine growing region, mostly light dry whites, some rosés
Savoyard, soupe	Usually with cheese and milk
Savoyarde, omelette	Omelette with cheese and fried potatoes
Scarole	Type of salad leaf
Scel-o-frais	Clingfilm
Schifela	Hot shoulder of smoked pork
Schwarzwurst	Pork and onion sausage
Scipion	Small cuttlefish
Scorpion	Name for spiny rascasse fish
Se plaindre	To complain
Seau à glace	Ice-bucket
Sébaste chèvré	Type of scorpion fish
Sec, sèche	Dry
Sèche	Sweet tart
Séguret	Red, rosé, and white from Côte du Rhône commune
Seiche	Cuttlefish
Seigle	Rye
Sel	Salt
Sel de table	Table salt
Sel gemme	Rock salt
Sel gris	Coarse rock or sea salt
Sel marin	Sea salt
Selle	Saddle, as lamb or veal
Selles-sur-cher	Blue-coated mild goats' cheese
Selon	According to
Selon arrivage	Available according to arrival
Selon grosseur (s.g.)	According to size

Seltz	Soda water
Semillon	White wine grape
Semoule	Semolina
Sénancole	Herbal liqueur
Sépia	Name for cuttlefish
Sepiole	Name for small cuttlefish
Sept yeux	Name for lamprey fish
Septmoncel	Thick round blue cows' cheese
Sériole	Amberjack fish
Serpolet	Wild thyme
Serran	Type of sea perch
Serran chevrette	Comber fish, similar grouper
Serre	Greenhouse
Serré	Solid whey cheese
Serré	Compact
Serveuse	Waitress
Servi, servie	Served
Service	Service
Service	Service charge
Service compris	Service charge included
Service non compris	Service not included
Serviette	Napkin
Sève	Sloe liqueur
Sèvre-et-Maine, Muscadet de, AC	The best of the Muscadets
Sevruga	Type of sturgeon and its caviar
Siège	Seat
Silure	Freshwater fish, similar turbot
Simple	Plain
Siouclet	Type of sandsmelt
Sirop	Syrup

Sirupeux	Syrupy, very sweet (as wine)
Six-yeux	Abalone
Smitane	Sour cream sauce
Sobronade	Thick pork, bean and vegetable soup
Socca	Chick pea fritter with salt and sugar
Soissonaise, à la	Usually with haricot beans
Soja	Soya
Sole	Dover sole
Sole pelouse	Sand sole
Sole pôlée	Sand sole
Sole tachetée	Speckled sole
Solette	Slip sole
Solférino, potage de	Thick garlicky tomato and vegetable soup
Solitaire	Very old wild boar
Sommelier	Wine waiter
Sorbe	Type of rowan apple
Sorbet	Water ice
Sot-l'y-laisse	Fleshy piece of chicken above parson's nose: a delicacy
Sou-fassoum	Cabbage stuffed with rich forcemeat
Soubise	With purée of onions
Soucoupe	Saucer
Soufflé	Light airy egg dish
Soumantrain	Smooth, spicy cows' cheese
Soupe	Soup, usually thick
Souper	Supper
Source	Spring
Souris	Knuckle of mutton
Sous	Under
Sous vide	In a sealed vacuum pack

Sous-noix	Cut of meat, especially veal
Spécialité	Speciality
Spoom	Juice or wine with egg whites
Squale	Name for dogfish
Squille	Type of shrimp
St Felicien	Firm salty cows' cheese
St Gildas des Bois	Rich soft creamy cows' cheese
St-Pourçain-sur-Sioule, VDQS	Country red, white and rosé wines from the upper Loire
STC	Service and tax included
Steack	Steak
Steack à point	Medium steak
Steack bien cuit	Well done steak
Steack bleu	Very rare steak
Steack haché	Ground steak, hamburger
Steack saignant	Rare steak
Steack tartare	Raw steak with egg, onions and capers
Stocaficada	Dried cod stewed with onions, tomatoes, garlic and basil
Stockfish	Dried flattened cod
Stoficado	Flattened dried cod
Subric	Small deep-fried croquette
Suc	Reduced consommé or meat juices
Sucette	Lollipop
Sucre	Sugar
Sucre brun	Brown sugar
Sucre cristallisé	Granulated sugar
Sucre de canne	Cane sugar
Sucre en morceaux	Sugar cubes
Sucre en poudre	Caster sugar

Sucre glacé	Icing sugar
Sucre roux	Brown sugar
Sucré, sucrée	Sweetened
Sucrin	Type of melon
Sud	South
Suédoise	Swedish-style
Suisse	Swiss
Suivant	Next, following
Suivant	According to; in the manner of
Supérieur	Higher, as in degree of alcohol
Supérieur	Better, superior
Supi	Name for cuttlefish
Suppion	Name for small cuttlefish
Suprême	Breast of poultry or game
Sur	On
Sur commande	On your order, as requested
Sur Lie, Muscadet, AC	Muscadet left lying on its lees or sediment for extra flavour
Sureau	Elderberry liqueur
Sureau	Elder tree
Surelle	Wild sorrel
Surfin, surfine	Extra fine
Surgelé	Frozen
Surprise	Surprise
Sus, en	In addition to
Suze	Spirit-based herbal aperitif
Suzette, crêpe	Pancake flambéed in orange liqueur
Sylvaner	White wine grape, especially Alsace
Syrah	Red wine grape, especially in Rhône

T.V.A.	V.A.T.
Table	Table
Table d'hôte	Fixed price meal with set menu
Table, vin de	Basic, everyday wine
Tablette	Small bar (as chocolate)
Tablier	Apron
Tablier de sapeur	Ox tripe in egg and breadcrumbs
Tacaud	Type of cod
Tacen	Term for a young salmon
Tâche, la, AC	Very superior red Burgundy from Côte de Nuits
Tamie	Firm mild pressed cows' cheese
Tanche	Tench, the fish
Tannat	Red wine grape from Southwestern France
Tapé, tapée	Dried, as fruit
Tapenade	Olive, anchovy and caper paste
Tapeno	A name for capers
Tapioca	Tapioca
Tarte tatin	Upside-down caramel apple tart
Tartare, sauce	Mayonnaise with capers, herbs, gherkin and garlic
Tarte	Tart, usually open

Tartelette	Small tart
Tartine	Slice of bread with butter or a spread
Tartiner, fromage à	Cheese spread
Tartinette	Sausage spread
Tartouffe	Potato
Tartouillat	Type of apple tart
Tassard	Kingfish
Tasse	Cup
Tassergal	Bluefish
Tastevin	Small flat silver tasting cup
Tatin, tarte	Upside-down apple tart
Tâtre des allymes	Onion tart
Taupe	Type of shark
Taupinière	Leaf-wrapped soft goats' cheese
Taureau	Bull
Tautenne	A name for squid
Tavel	Good rosé wine from Rhône
Telline	Small clam
Tendre de tranche	Topside of beef
Tendron	Small cut of meat
Tergoule	Rice pudding
Terreux	Earthy (especially wine)
Terrine	Covered earthenware dish
Terrine	Name for a cooked pâté
Tête	Head
Tête d'aloyau	Cut of beef sirloin from rump
Tête de cuvée	The best casks of the vintage
Tête de mort	Nickname for Dutch edam cheese
Tête de nègre	Type of mushroom
Tête de veau	Boiled calf's head
Tête, fromage de	Brawn

Tétine	Udder
Téton de vénus	Type of peach
Tétragone	Type of spinach
Tétras	Grouse
Thé	Tea
Thé au citron	Tea with lemon
Thé au lait	Tea with milk
Théière	Teapot
Thermidor, homard	Lobster cooked in shell with thick sauce, grilled with cheese
Thiézac	Strong blue mould cows' cheese
Thionville	Strong-tasting processed cheese
Thon	Tuna
Thon rouge	Bluefin tuna
Thonine	Small tuna
Thonne	Style of cooking veal with tunafish
Thouarsais, VDQS	Light red, white rosé from Loire
Thourins	Thick milk and onion soup
Thym	Thyme
Thym-citron	Lemon thyme
Tian	Shallow cooking dish
Tiède	Warm
Tilleul	Lime tree
Tilleul, infusion de	Herbal tea of limeflowers
Timbale	Round dish or mould
Tintaine	Anise-flavoured liqueur
Tioro	Fish stew with garlic and tomatoes
Tirage, liqueur de	Sugar and alcohol mix added to sparkling wines

Tire	A name for skate
Tire-bouchon	Corkscrew
Tirer sur lie	Taken straight from the lees
Tisane	Herb tea
Tisane de champagne	Term for a very light champagne
Tocane	Term for champagne from first pressing
Toilette	Lavatory
Tokay d'Alsace	White wine grape from Alsace
Tomate	Tomato
Tomato de mer	Type of sea-anenome
Tomme	Type of round pressed cheese usually goats' or ewes'
Tomme de camargue	Thick round fresh soft sheep's cheese
Tomme de cantal	Thick round flesh soft cows' cheese
Tomme de Mont Ventoux	Round soft mild creamy ewes' cheese
Tomme de savoie	Firm, round, flat nutty cows' cheese
Tonneau en chêne	Oak-barrel
Topinambour	Jerusalem artichoke
Torchon	Napkin
Torpille	Large skate
Torte	Rich cream cake
Tortue	Turtle
Tortue de mer	Green sea turtle
Tortue luth	Giant sea turtle
Tortue, herbes à	Herbs for soup: basil, thyme, bay and marjoram
Tôt-fait	Quick lemon sponge
Tôtelots	Noodles in a vinaigrette

Touffe	Stalks (especially herbs), tied in a bunch
Toupin	Cooking pot
Tourain	Onion soup, bread and grated cheese
Touraine	Loire region, mostly white wines, some red, rosé
Tourangelle, à la	Touraine-style; often with beans
Tourmeta	Ewes' cheese pastry
Tournedos	Small round fillet steak
Tournesol	Sunflower
Tournesol, huile de	Sunflower seed oil
Tournon St Pierre	Tangy soft goats' cheese
Tourte	Pie
Tourteau	Large crab
Tourtière	Pie dish
Tourtou	Buckwheat pancake
Tous, tout, toutes	All, every
Toute-épice	Allspice
Train	Hindquarters
Train de boeuf	Rib of beef
Traiteur	Delicatessen
Traminer	White wine grape, especially Alsace
Tranche	Thick slice
Tranquille	Non-sparkling
Trappiste	General name for cheeses made by monks
Trappistine	Brandy-based herb liqueur
Travers de porc	Spareribs of pork
Trébuc	Potted meat, usually goose, duck, turkey or pork
Tremble	Large skate
Trempette	Bread soaked in soup

Trenouls	Lambs' tripe with wine and tomatoes
Tricholome	Variety of mushroom
Trinquer	To clink glasses
Tripailles	Tripe
Tripe de mer	Octopus
Tripée	Pigs' tripe stewed in white wine
Tripes	Tripe
Tripettes	A name for sheep's tripe
Triple-sec	Clear orange-flavoured liqueur
Triple-crème	Cheese with at least 75 per cent fat
Tripoux	Stuffed sheep's feet
Trompette des morts	Type of mushroom
Tronçon	Thick slice
Troo	Mild, nutty goats' cheese
Trop cher	Too expensive
Trou	Sorbet served between courses
Trou Normand	Calvados sorbet
Trouffe	Potato
Trousseau	Red wine grape, especially in Jura
Troyes	Soft round creamy cows' cheese
Trucha	Spinach omelette
Truche	Term for potato
Truffade	Cheesy potato fritter
Truffe	Truffle
Truffé, truffée	Garnished with truffles
Truite	Trout

Truite au bleu	Very fresh trout cooked quickly in vinegar-based fish stock
Truite de Dieppe	Salmon trout
Truite de mer	Salmon trout
Truite rivière	Brown trout
Truite arc-en-ciel	Rainbow trout
Trulet	Black pudding of pork and vegetables
Trulle	Rich black pudding with rice and cream
Trumeau	Shin of beef
Tuile	Small thin curved almond biscuit
Tulipe	Tulip-shaped glass, often with ice-cream or mousse
Turban	Ring-shaped
Turbot	Turbot
Turbot lisse	A name for brill
Turbotin	Small turbot
Turque, à la	Turkish-style
Tursan, VDQS	Red, dry white, rosé from Landes in Southwestern France

Ugni blanc	White wine grape, especially Southern France
Urval	Grape-related
Urval, station d'	Fresh grapejuice counter
Uzès, sauce d'	Usually with anchovy and madeira

Vaccarese	Red wine grape, especially Rhône valley
Vachard	Strong round cows' cheese
Vache	Cow
Vacherin	Meringue with cream, ice-cream
Vacherin	Soft round cows' cheese usually wrapped in pine bark
Vacherin d'abondance	Soft mild flat cows' cheese
Vacherin des Bauges	Pink-coated runny cows' cheese
Vacherin mont d'or	Mild creamy soft cows' cheese
Vachotte	Type of mushroom
Vacqueyras	Full reds, rosés, few whites from Rhône valley commune
Vairon	Minnow
Vaiselle	Crockery
Vaiselle	Washing-up
Valençay	Soft mild pyramid goats' cheese
Valençay, VDQS	Light reds and dry whites from Loire
Valence	Spanish orange
Valois	Usually with artichokes and potatoes
Valréas	Red wines from Côtes du Rhône appellation

Vanette	Scallop
Vanille	Vanilla
Vanilline	Artificial vanilla flavouring
Vanneau	Queen scallop
Vapeur	Steam
Varié	Assorted
Vasque	Shallow bowl, especially for desserts
Vaucluse	Rhône valley region: mostly reds and rosés
VDN	Vin doux naturel: natural sweet wine
VDP	Vin de pays: country wines, cut above table wine, below VDQS
VDQS	Vin delimité, qualité superieur: below AC but better than VDP
VDT	Vin de table
Veau	Veal
Velouté	Smooth creamy white sauce
Venaison	Venison
Vendange	Annual harvest of grapes
Vendange tardive	Late harvested wine
Vendôme	Firm, ash-coated ewes' cheese
Ventre	Belly
Ventrèche	Smoked breast of pork
Ventrise	Salted breast of pork
Verdette	Type of mushroom
Verdure	Green vegetables
Verdurette	Vinaigrette with fresh herbs
Verdurière	Usually with lots of green leaves or fresh herbs

Verjus	Tart juice of unripe grapes used as vinegar
Verjus, clarequets de	Grapejuice jelly
Vermicelle	Vermicelli noodles
Vermouth	Wine-based aperitif flavoured with herbs and wormwood
Verni	Smooth venus clam
Véronique	Usually with grapes
Verre	A glass
Vert bonnet	Type of mushroom
Vert pré	Usually green garnish including peas, bean
Vert, verte	Green
Verte	Name for green oyster from Marenne
Verte, sauce	Mayonnaise with fresh herbs
Verveine	Verbena, the plant
Verveine du Velay	Verbena-flavoured liqueur
Vessie	Bladder of pig
Vestiaire	Cloakroom
Vézelay	Soft strong conical goats' cheese with blue rind
Viande	Meat
Vichy	Type of sparkling mineral water
Vichyssoise	Chilled leek and potato soup
Vide	Empty
Vieille	Old
Vieille	Wrasse
Vieille cure	Brandy-based herb liqueur
Vieille réserve	Denotes aged spirit
Vieille tête	Strong-smelling pickled cows' cheese
Vieillissement	Aging (of wine)

Viennoise	Viennese-style: usually fried in egg and breadcrumbs
Vierge	Virgin, as olive oil
Vierge	Frothy lemon butter
Vieux	Old
Vigne	A grape vine
Vigneau	Winkle
Vigneron, vigneronne	Wine grower
Vigneronne, à la	Usually with grapes, vine-leaves or wine
Vignoble	Vineyard
Villages	Villages
Vin	Wine
Vin blanc	White wine
Vin blanc cassis	White wine, blackcurrant liqueur
Vin bourru	New, as yet unfiltered wine
Vin chaud	Mulled wine
Vin cuit	Homemade dessert wine
Vin de café	Light, easy drinking red wine
Vin de carafe	Everyday drinking wine
Vin de comptoir	Everyday drinking wine
Vin de consommation courante	Everyday drinking wine
Vin de coule	Wine from first grape pressing
Vin de garde	Wine which should be kept to age
Vin de goutte	Wine from last grape pressing
Vin de liqueur	Very sweet wine
Vin de paille	Wine from grapes dried on straw

Vin de palus	Wine grown on salt marshes
Vin de pays	Country wine: a step below VDQS
Vin de plaine	Wine from the flat, said to be inferior to wine from slope
Vin de presse	Wine made from grape residue
Vin de primeur	Very young wine
Vin de queue	Wine from pressed grape stalks
Vin de sables	Wine grown on the sands
Vin de table	Unclassified ordinary wine
Vin de tête	Wine from first pressing
Vin doux	Sweet wine
Vin doux naturel	Sweet wine fortified with brandy
Vin gris	Very pale rosé wine, almost grey
Vin jaune	Pale yellow wine, usually from Jura
Vin liquoreux	Very sweet white wine
Vin mousseux	Sparkling wine
Vin nature	Unsweetened wine
Vin nouveau	Young wine, less than a year old
Vin rosé	Rosé wine
Vin rouge	Red wine
Vin vert	Crisp young white from Midi
Vinaigre	Vinegar
Vinaigrette	Cold sauce of oil, vinegar and seasonings
Vinificateur	Wine-maker
Vinsobres	Full reds from eastern Rhône
Viognier	A white wine grape

Violet	Sea fig, small edible sea creature
Violet	Purple
Violette	Violet
Violette, crème de	Violet-perfumed liqueur
Violon	Skate
Virgouleuse	Pear
Visan	Full reds, rosé and white from Côte du Rhône commune
Visitandine	Small cake
Vitelotte	Potato
Viticole	Wine-related
Viticulteur	Wine-grower
Vittel	Type of still mineral water
Vive	Weever fish
Vive araignée	Type of weever fish
Vive rayée	Striped weever fish
Viveur	Usually very spicy, very peppery dish
Vivier	Fish tank
VO	Denotes age of spirit, very old
Voiture	Trolley for cheeses and/or desserts
Vol-au-vent	Puff pastry case
Volaille	Poultry
Volnay, AC	Very good red burgundies from Côte de Beaune
Volnay-Santenots, AC	Good red burgundies from Meursault in the Côte de Beaune
Volvic	Type of still mineral water
Vosgienne, à la	Usually with plums

Vosne-romanée, AC	Superior red burgundies from Côte de Nuits
Vougeot, AC	Very good red Burgundy from Côte de Nuits
Vouvray, AC	Light dry still or sparkling white from Loire
Voves cendré	Soft mild cows' cheese, ash-coated
Vras	Wrasse fish similar to sea perch
Vrille de vigne	Vine tendrils, often pickled
VS, VSOP	Denotes aged spirit, especially brandy

Waldorf, salade	Chicken and walnut salad
Walewska, sole	With truffles, lobster and cheese sauce
Waterzooi	Stew of freshwater fish
Whisky	Whisky
Williams, poire	Clear spirit of Williams pear
Williams, poire	Type of pear
Witloof	Chicory

Xavier, potage de	Rich creamy rice soup with chicken garnish
Xérès	Sherry
XO	Denotes age of cognac, extra old

Yaourt	Yoghurt
York, jambon de	Cooked ham
Yvette, pommes	Strips of potato baked in butter

Zébrine	Type of aubergine
Zephir	Light frothy dish, usually dessert
Zeste	Peel or rind of citrus fruits
Zinc	Bar or counter
Zingara	Gypsy-style: usually with ham, tongue, mushrooms and truffles
Ziste	White pith of citrus fruits
Zizi	Champagne, blackcurrant and raspberry cocktail

Abalone	Ormeau, ormier, oreille de mer f
According to	Suivant, selon
Acid	Acidulé
Addition, in; on top of	Sus, en
Advice	Conseil m
After-taste	Arrière-goût m
Alcohol	Alcool m
All	Tout, toute, tous, toutes
Allspice	Toute-épice f
Almond	Amande f
Almond, caramelised	Praslin m
Alsatian-style	Alsaciènne, à l'
Amberjack	Liche f, sériole f
Anchovy	Anchois m
Anchovy and garlic paste	Anchoiade m
Anchovy and hot oil dip	Bagna cauda f
Anchovy purée	Pissalat m
Angel	Ange m
Angelica	Angélique f
Angel's hair (pasta)	Cheveux d'ange m
Anglerfish	Baudroie f
Animal, wild	Fauve m
Aniseed	Anis m

Appetiser	Amuse-gueule f, amusette f
Apple	Pomme f
Apple, pippin	Reinette f
Apple, Cox	Reine des reinettes f
Apricot	Abricot m
Apron	Tablier m
Aromatic	Aromatique
Artichoke	Artichaut m
Artichoke bottom	Fond d'artichaut m
Ash	Cendre f
Ashtray	Cendrier m
Asparagus	Asperge f
Ass	Ânesse f
Assorted	Varié
Aubergine	Aubergine f
Aubergine stew	Barbouillade f
Available (if arrived)	Selon arrivage
Avocado	Avocat m

English	French
Bacon rasher	Lardon m
Bacon, packaged	Bacon m
Baked	Four, au
Bakery	Boulangerie f
Ball	Ballon m
Ball, small	Boulette f
Balm	Baume m
Bamboo	Bambou m
Banana	Banane f
Bar	Bar m
Bar (counter)	Zinc m
Bar (as chocolate)	Tablette f
Barbel	Barbeau m
Barding bacon	Barde f
Barley	Orge f
Barnacle	Patelle f, barnache f
Barnacle, goose-necked	Pouce-pied m
Barracuda	Brochet de mer m
Barrel, of wine	Barrique f
Base	Fond m
Basil	Basilic m
Basil paste or sauce	Pistou m
Basket	Corbeille f
Basket	Panier m
Bass	Cernier m
Baste, to	Juter

Baste or moisten, to	Arroser
Batter	Pâte à frire m
Bayleaf	Feuille de laurier f
Beak	Bec m
Bean, runner	Haricot d'espagne m
Bean, broad	Fève f
Bean, dried	Haricot m
Bean, green kidney	Flageolet m
Bean, kidney	Faséole f
Bean, red kidney	Haricot rouge m
Bean, runner	Haricot grimpant m
Bean, small broad	Féverole f
Bean, string or French	Haricot vert m
Bean, white haricot	Haricot blanc m
Beast	Bête f
Beaten or whipped	Battu
Bed	Lit m
Beechnut	Faine f
Beef	Boeuf m
Beef stew	Boeuf à la bourguignonne m
Beef (topside)	Tendre de tranche f
Beef, rib of	Train de boeuf m
Beef, rump	Tête d'aloyau f
Beef, shoulder of	Macreuse
Beef, sirloin	Contre-filet m
Beef, skirt of	Bavette f
Beefsteak	Biftek m
Beehive	Rûche f
Beer	Bière f
Beer, homebrewed	Bière de menage f
Beermug	Chope f
Beetroot	Betterave f

Belly	Ventre m
Berry	Baie f
Berry or bean (as coffee)	Grain m
Better, superior	Meilleur, superieur
Big	Gros, grosse
Bilberry	Myrtille f
Bill	Addition f
Bill (slang)	Ardoise f
Bird	Oiseau m
Biscuit	Biscuit m
Biscuit, almond	Tuile f
Biscuit, boudoir	Langue de chat f
Biscuit, crisp	Croquet m
Biscuit, macaroon	Ratafia f, macaron, m
Bitter	Amer, amère
Black	Noir, noire
Black pudding	Boudin noir m
Blackberry	Mûre sauvage, mûre de ronce f
Blackberry bush	Ronce f, mûrier, m
Blackcurrant	Cassis m
Blackcurrant liqueur	Cassis, crème de f
Bladder, of pig	Vessie f
Blanched	Émondé
Bleeding	Saignant, saignante
Blend	Coupage m
Blenny	Baveuse f
Bloater	Craquelot m
Blood	Sang m
Blood, cooked	Sanguette f
Bluefish	Tassergal m
Boar, baby	Bête rousse f

Boar, old	Sanglier m
Boar, young	Marcassin m
Boiled	Bouilli, bouillie
Boiling	Bouillant
Bone	Os m
Bone marrow	Moelle f
Boned	Désossé
Bonito tuna	Pelamide f
Borage	Bourrache f
Border	Bordure f
Bottle	Bouteille f
Bottle-opener	Décapsuleur m
Bottled	Mis en bouteilles
Bottom, of joint	Cul m
Bottoms up!	Cul sec!
Bowl	Bol m, écuelle f
Bowl or basin (large)	Vasque f
Brains	Cervelles f plural
Braised	Braisé, braisée
Bran bread	Pain de son m
Brand	Marque f
Brandy, fine	Cognac m
Brawn	Fromage de tête m
Brawn, pig's	Hure, de porc f
Brazil nut	Noix du Brésil f
Bread	Pain m
Bread roll	Pain, petit m
Bread, brown	Pain bis m
Bread, fried	Crôuton m
Bread, large loaf	Gros pain m
Bread, long white	Baguette f
Bread, plaited loaf	Natte f
Bread, ring loaf	Couronne f
Bread, rye	Pain de seigle m

Bread, thin loaf	Flûte f
Bread, toasted	Pain grillé m
Bread, wholemeal	Pain complet m
Bread, wholemeal	Pain entier m
Breadcrumbed	Pané
Breadcrumbs	Chapelure f, panure f
Breadstick	Longuet m, gressin m
Breakfast	Petit déjeuner m
Breakfast, continental	Café complet m
Bream, black	Griset m
Bream, freshwater	Brème f
Bream, gilt-head	Daurade f
Bream, Mediterranean	Pagre m
Bream, Red Sea	Dorade f
Bream, sea	Brème de mer f
Breast	Poitrine f
Breast, of poultry	Suprême f
Brill	Barbue f
Brine	Saumure f
Broad	Large
Broccoli	Brocoli m
Broom plant	Petit-houx m
Broth	Bouillon m
Broth (as soup)	Brouet m
Broth, poaching	Court-bouillon m
Brown	Brun, brune
Brown sugar	Cassonade f
Brussel sprouts	Choux de bruxelles m
Buckwheat	Blé noir m, sarrasin m
Buckwheat porridge	Far m
Bull	Taureau m
Bun, spicy	Moque f

Burbot	Lotte de rivière f
Burdock	Bardane f
Burgundy	Bourgogne f
Burned	Brûlé, brûlée
Burnet	Pimpernelle f
Bustard	Outarde f
Butcher's shop	Boucherie f
Butter	Beurre m
Butterbean	Haricot beurre, haricot jaune m
Butterdish	Beurrier m
Buttered	Embeurré
Buttermilk	Babeurre m, lait barratté m

Cabbage, cabbages	Chou m, choux m plural
Cabbage, pickled	Choucroute m
Cabbage, red	Chou-rouge m
Café, transport	Relais routiers m
Cake	Gâteau m
Cake, cream	Torte f
Cake, small sponge	Madeleine f
Camomile	Camomille f
Candle	Bougie f
Candyfloss	Barbe-à-papa f
Capers	Câpres f
Carafe	Carafe f
Caraway	Carvi m
Carbonated	Gazeux, gaseuse
Cardamom	Cardamome f
Carnation	Oeillet m
Carob	Caroube m
Carp	Carpe f
Carrot	Carotte f
Cashdesk, cashier	Caisse f
Cashew	Cajou m, anacarde f
Catfish	Loup marin m
Cauldron	Chaudron m
Cauliflower	Chou-fleur m
Caviar	Caviar m
Celeriac	Céleri-rave m

Celery	Céleri m
Celery, wild	Ache f
Cellar	Cave f
Cellar, wine	Chai m
Cellarman	Caviste m
Cellarmaster	Maître de chai m
Cereal	Céréale f
Chair	Chaise f
Champagne	Champagne m
Char	Omble chevalier m
Charcoal	Charbon m
Chard	Blette f
Cheaper	Moins cher
Cheek	Joue f
Cheek, of pig	Bajoue f
Cheers	Santé, à votre
Cheese	Fromage m
Cheesecake	Fromaget m
Cheesespread	Fromage à tartiner m
Cheesestraw	Pailette dorée f
Cherry	Cerise f
Cherry, wild	Merise f
Cherry, bitter	Griotte f
Cherry brandy	Guignolet m
Chervil	Cerfeuil m
Chestnut	Marron m, châtaigne f
Chestnut, crystallised	Marron glacé m
Chicken breast	Blanc de volaille m
Chicken wingtips	Ailerons m
Chicken, capon	Chapon m
Chicken, free-range	Poulet fermier, poulet jaune m
Chicken, maize-fed	Poulet de bresse m

Chicken, pullet	Poulette f
Chicken, roasting	Poularde f
Chicken, small spring	Petit poussin m
Chicken, spring	Poussin m
Chicken, young	Poulet m
Chickpeas	Pois chiches m
Chicory	Chicon m, endive f
Chicory root	Chicorée à café f
Chicory, wild	Barbe-de-capucin f
Chilli	Piment fort rouge m
Chilled (as wine)	Frais
Chine, of meat	Échine f
Chinese leaf	Chou de chine m
Chips	Frites f
Chives	Ciboulette f
Chocolate	Chocolat m
Chocolate, cooking	Chocolat à cuire m
Chocolate, fine cooking	Couverture f
Chocolate, powder	Chocolat en poudre m
Choice	Choix m
Chop, rib	Côte f
Chopsticks	Baguettes f
Christmas	Noël m
Chub fish	Chevaine f, chevesne m
Chump	Quasi m
Cider	Cidre m
Cinnamon	Cannelle f
Clam	Praire f, verni m, palourde f
Clam, razor shell	Couteau m
Clam, small	Clovisse f
Clams, stuffed	Palourdes farcies f

Claw	Pince f
Clean, to	Débarraser
Clingfilm	Scel-o-frais m
Clink glasses, to	Trinquer les verres
Cloakroom	Vestiaire m
Clog	Sabot m
Closed	Fermé
Closing	Fermeture f
Clove	Girofle m
Coalfish	Merluche noire f
Cockerel	Coq m
Cockerel	Coquelet m
Cock	Coque f, bucard m
Cockscomb	Crête de coq f
Cocoa	Cacao m
Coconut	Noix de coco f
Coconutmilk	Lait de coco m
Cod	Cabillaud m
Cod, dried	Estoficado m
Cod, salted and puréed	Brandade de morue f
Codling	Colineau m
Coffee	Café m
Coffee without milk	Café nature m
Coffee, beans	Café en grains m
Coffee, decaffeinated	Faux-café m
Coffee, ground	Café moulu m
Coffee, instant	Café en poudre m
Coffee, small with cream	Café crème m
Coffee, with hot milk	Café au lait m
Coffee, with ice-cream	Café liègoise m

Cold	Froid, froide
Coley	Lieu noir m
Compact	Serré
Complain, to	Se plaindre
Complaint	Protestation f, plainte f
Condiments	Assaisonnement m
Confectionery	Confiserie f
Conger eel	Congre m
Connoisseur, of food	Gourmet m
Continental breakfast	Café complet m
Cooked	Cuit
Cooking	Cuisine f
Cool	Frais, fraîche
Cooling	Rafraîchissant
Cool or iced drink	Frappé
Copper	Cuivre m
Coral, as in shellfish	Corail m
Coriander	Coriandre m
Cork	Bouchon m
Corked (as wine)	Bouchonné
Corkscrew	Tire-bouchon m
Corncob	Papeton m
Cornet	Cornet m
Cornflake	Flocon de mais m
Cornflour	Fleur de mais f, amidon de blé m
Country	Campagne f
Country	Pays m
Country-style	Campagnard
Courgette	Courgette f
Cover, cover charge	Couvert m
Cover, for dish	Cloche f
Cow	Vache f

Crab	Crabe m
Crab, large	Tourteau m
Cracker	Craquelin m
Crackling	Cretons m, gratton, m
Cranberry	Canneberge f, airelle rouge f
Crayfish	Écrevisse f
Crazy	Fou
Cream	Crème f
Cream caramel	crème caramel f, flan m
Cream, whipped	Crème fouettée f
Credit cards	Cartes de credit f
Cress	Cressonette f
Crisp, crusty	Croustillant
Crockery	Vaisselle f
Crowfish	Corb m
Crown	Couronne f
Crunchy	Croquant
Crushed	Concassé
Crust, as topping	Croûte f
Crust, bread	Grignon m
Crustaceans	Crustaces m
Crystallised, preserved	Confit
Cucumber	Concombre m
Cucumbers, salted	Agoursi m
Cumin	Cumin m
Cumin, sweet	Anis vert m
Cup	Tasse f
Cup, small	Demi-tasse f
Curds, of milk	Lait caillé, m
Curry	Cari, kari m
Custard	Crème anglaise f
Cutlery	Coutellerie f

Cutlet	Côtelette f
Cuttlefish	Seiche f
Cuttlefish, small	Suppion m, sépiole f

Dab	Limande f
Dainty	Mignon
Dairy	Laiterie f
Dairy products	Laitages m
Dandelion	Pissenlit, grouin d'âne m
Date	Datte f
Day	Jour m
De-fatted	Dégraissé
Decaffeinated coffee	Café décateiné m
Decant	Décanter
Deer, red	Cerf m
Delicatessen	Traiteur m, charcutier m
Dessert	Dessert m
Dessert course	Entremets m
Devilled	Diable, à la
Diced	Dés, en
Diet	Régime m
Diet, on a	Régime, au
Dill	Aneth f
Diluted	Allongé
Dine, to; (also dinner)	Dîner, (dîné m)
Dish, small pottery	Cassolette f
Dish, of the day	Plat du jour m
Dish, small	Cocotte f
Doe	Biche f

Dogfish	Baudroise f, petite rousette f
Dolphin	Dauphin m
Dolphin fish	Coriphène f
Donkey	Âne m
Dory, John	Saint-pierre m
Double	Double
Draught beer	Bière pression f
Dried (as fruit)	Sec, sèche
Drink	Boisson m
Drink (before meal)	Aperitif m
Drink (after dinner)	Digestif m
Drinkable (as water)	Potable
Drinking water	Eau potable f
Drop	Goutte f
Drumstick	Pilon m
Drunk	Ivre, éméché
Dry	Sec, sèche
Dry, very (as wine)	Extra-sec
Duck	Canard m
Duck breast	Maïgret m, magret m
Duck, barbary	Canard de barbarie m
Duck, smoked fillet	Rougeot m
Duck, spoonbill	Bec-plat m
Duck, young	Canardeau m
Duckling	Caneton m, canette f
Dumpling	Quenelle f, noque f
Dumpling, maize	Mique f
Dumplings, buckwheat	Pouloud m
Dutch	Hollandais

Ear	Oreille f
East	Est
Easter	Pâques f
Eel	Anguille f
Eel, small	Anguillette f
Eels, baby	Civelles f
Egg	Oeuf m
Egg white	Blanc d'oeuf
Egg yolk	Jaune d'oeuf
Egg, Easter	Oeuf de Pâques m
Egg, new laid	Oeuf du jour m
Egg-timer	Sablier m
Eggcup	Coquetier m
Eggnog	Lait de poule m
Eggs, fried	Oeufs à la poêle, oeuf au plat
Elder tree	Sureau m
Empty	Vide
English-style	Anglaise, à l'
Espresso	Express m
Espresso, strong	Café serré m
Essence	Essence f
Every	Tout, toute
Ewe	Brebis f
Ewe, lamb	Agnelle f
Expensive	Cher
Expensive, too	Trop cher
Extract	Extrait m

Faggot	Caillette
False	Faux, fausse
Family, family style	Famille f
Farm	Ferme f
Fat, lard	Graisse
Fatty	Gras, grasse
Fawn	Faon m
Fennel	Fenouil m
Fig	Figue f
Figpecker bird	Becfigue m
Fillet	Filet m
Filter coffee	Café filtre m
Fin	Nageoire f
Fine	Fin, fine
Fir tree	Sapin m
Fire	Feu m
First	Primeur
Fish	Poisson m
Fish fry	Alevin m, poissonaille f
Fish soup	Soupe de poisson f
Fish tank	Vivier m
Fishbone	Arête f
Fisherman	Pêcheur m
Fishkettle	Poissonière f
Fishmonger	Poissonnier m
Fishmonger's	Poissonerie f
Fish stew	Chaudrée f, cotriade f

Fixed	Fixe
Fixed price	Prix fixe m
Flake	Flocon m
Flamed	Flambé
Flank	Flanchet m, plat-de-côtes m
Flank of beef	Onglet m
Flat	Plat, plate
Flavour	Parfum m
Flesh	Chair f
Flounder	Flet m
Flour	Farine f
Flower	Fleur f
Flying fish	Poisson volant m
Food	Alimentation f
Foot	Pied m
Fork	Fourchette f
Fortified wine	Vin doux naturel
Free	Gratuit, gratuite
Fresh	Frais, fraîche
Fried	Frit, frite
Fried egg	Oeuf frit m
Fritter	Beignet m, fritot m
Frivolous	Folle
Frog	Grenouille f
Frogs' legs	Cuisses de grenouille f
Frosted	Givré
Frozen	Surgelé
Fruit	Fruit m
Fruity (as wine)	Fruité
Frying pan	Poêle f
Full	Complet
Full-bodied (wine)	Corsé, charnu

Game	Gibier m
Gamey, high	Faisandé
Garfish	Aiguille f, orphie f
Garlic	Ail m
Garlic (plural)	Aulx m
Garlic sauce	Aillade f, aioli m
Garnish	Garniture f
Garnished	Garni
Gelatine	Gélatine f
Gherkin	Cornichon m
Giblets	Abbatis m
Gin	Genièvre m, gin
Ginger	Gingembre m
Gingerbeer	Bière de gingembre f
Gingerbread	Pain d'épice m
Gizzard	Gésier m
Glass	Verre m
Glass dish	Coupe f
Glaze (as sauce)	Glace f
Goat	Chèvre f
Gold	Or m
Golden	Doré
Good	Bon, bonne
Goose	Oie f
Gooseberry	Groseille à maquereau f
Gosling	Oison m
Goulash	Gulyas f

Grain	Grain m
Grape	Grain de raisin m
Grape	Raisin m, grain de raisin m
Grape jam	Raisiné f
Grapefruit	Pamplemousse m
Grapevine	Cépage m, vigne f
Grated	Râpé, râpée
Gravy	Jus de viande m
Greaseproof paper	Papier sulfurisé m
Great	Grand, grande
Greek	Grecque, à la
Green	Vert, verte
Greengage	Reine-claude f
Greengrocer's shop	Fruiterie f
Greenhouse	Serre f
Grey	Gris, grise
Grey mullet	Muge f
Grill	Grillade f
Grilled, toasted	Grillé, grillée
Grocer's shop	Épicerie f
Ground	Moulu, moulue; en poudre
Grouper	Mérou m
Grouse	Grouse f, coq de bruyère m
Growth (as wine)	Cru m
Guava	Goyave f
Guest	Invité, invitée; hôte, m
Guinea fowl	Pintade f
Guinea fowl, young	Pintadeau m
Gurnard	Grondin m
Gurnard, streaked	Grondin imbragio m

Haddock	Aiglefin m, églefin m
Hake	Colin m, merlue, merluche, f
Half	Demi m, moitié f
Half-bottle	Demi-bouteille f, fillette f
Halibut	Flétan m
Ham	Jambon m
Ham, cooked	Jambon blanc m, jambon de York m
Ham, cured	Jambon de bayonne m
Ham, cured country	Jambon de pays m
Ham, whole small	Jambonneau m
Hamburger	Steack haché; boeuf haché m
Hard	Dur
Hard-boiled egg	Oeuf dur m
Hare	Lièvre m
Hare, young	Levraut m
Harvest	Récolte f
Harvested	Récolté
Harvest, grape	Vendanges f
Haunch	Cimier m
Haunch	Gigue f
Hawthorn	Aubépine f
Hay	Foin m
Hazelnut	Aveline f, noisette f
Head	Tête f
Head, calf's	Tête de veau f
Headwaiter	Maître d'hotel m

Health	Santé f
Heap, in a	Buisson, en
Heart	Coeur m
Hedgehog	Hérisson m
Heifer	Génisse f
Hen	Poule f
Herb	Herbe f
Herb tea	Infusion f
Herbs, bunch of	Bouquet garni m
Herbs, mixed fresh	Fines herbes f
Hermit-crab	Bernard l'ermite m
Herring	Hareng m
Herring, salted and smoked	Saur m
Herring, small baltic	Baltique m
High	Haut, haute
Hillside	Côte f
Hindquarters	Train m
Holly	Houx m
Honey	Miel m
Honeycomb	Rayon de miel m
Hop	Houblon m
Hop shoot	Houblon, jet d' m
Horse, horse-meat	Cheval m
Horseradish	Raifort m, moutardelle f
Hostess	Hôtesse f
Hot	Chaud
Hôtel	Hôtel m
House	Maison f
House-special	Maison, spécialité de la f
Hungarian	Hongroise
Hunger	Faim m
Hungry, to be	Faim, avoir

Hurry, in a	Pressé
Huss	Grande roussette f
Hyssop	Hysope f

Ice	Glace f
Ice, water	Sorbet m
Ice-bucket	Seau à glace m
Ice-cream	Glace f
Ice-cube	Glaçon m
Iced	Frappé
Iced, frozen	Glacé, glacée
Iced coffee	Café glacé m
Icing	Glaçage m
Included	Compris
Inedible	Inmangeable
Ink	Encre f
Inn	Auberge f, hôtellerie f, relais m
Instead of	Au lieu de
Irish coffee	Café gallois m

Jam	Confiture f
Jelly, aspic	Gelée f
Jewish	Juif, juive
Juice	Jus m
Juicy	Juteux, juteuse
Juniper	Genièvre m

Kernel	Noyau m
Kettle	Bouilloire f
Kid	Chevreau m, cabri m, broutard m
Kidney	Rognon m
King	Roi m
Kingfish	Tassard m
Kitchen	Cuisine f
Knife	Couteau m
Kohl rabi	Chou-rave m
Kosher	Cachir, kachir

Label, of wine	Étiquette
Lake	Lac m
Lamb	Agneau m
Lamb, baby	Agnelet, m
Lamb, milk-fed	Agneau de lait m
Lamb, salt marsh	Agneau de pré-salé m
Lamprey	Lamproie m
Landlord	Hôte m
Lard	Saindoux m
Larded	Piqué
Lark	Alouette f
Late	En retard
Laurel	Laurier m
Lavatory	Toilettes f
Leaf	Feuille f
Leaf, small (as herb)	Pluche f
Lean, thin	Maigre
Leek	Poireau m
Lees, of wine	Lie f
Left-overs	Restes m
Leg, of lamb	Gigot m
Lemon	Citron m
Lemon drink, fresh	Citron pressé m
Lemon liqueur	Citronnelle f
Lemon thyme	Thym-citron m
Lemonade	Limonade f
Lemon balm	Mélisse f

Lemon sole	Limande f
Lemon squash	Citronnade f
Lentil	Lentille f
Lettuce	Laitue f
Lettuce, cos	Laitue romaine f
Lettuce, curly or frizzy	Chicorée frisée f, frisée f
Lettuce, iceberg	Reine des glaces f
Lettuce, lamb's	Mâche f, doucette f
Lettuce, round soft	Laitue beurrée f
Light (as wine)	Lèger
Lime	Citron vert m, limon m
Lime tree	Tilleul m
Limpet	Patelle f, barnache f, bernique f
Ling	Lingue f
Liqueur	Liqueur f
Liquorice	Réglisse f
Liver	Foie m
Liver, calf's	Foie de veau m
Loach	Loche f
Lobster	Homard m
Lobster, flat	Cigale f
Lobster, spiny	Langouste f
Local	Régional, local
Log	Bûche f
Loin	Longe f
Lollipop	Sucette f
Long	Long, longue
Long-life milk	Lait sterilisé m
Lorry driver	Routier m
Lovage	Livèche f
Low	Bas, basse

Lumpfish	Lièvre de mer m, lompe f
Lunch	Déjeuner m
Lungs, lights	Mou m

Macaroni	Macaroni m
Macaroon	Macaron m
Mace	Macis m
Macerated	Macéré
Mackerel	Maquereau m
Mackerel, chub	Maquereau espagnol m
Mackerel, horse	Saurel m
Madeira	Madère f
Maderised	Maderisé
Main course	Plat principal m, entrée f
Maize	Maïs m
Maize, cooked	Polente f, armotte f
Marjoram	Marjolaine f
Mallowplant	Mauve f
Malmsey	Malvoisie, vin de m
Manager	Gérant m
Mango	Mangue f
Manner, in the	Façon, à la
Maraschino cherry	Marasquin m
Marinated	Mariné, marinée
Market garden	Marais m
Marmalade	Confiture d'orange f
Marrow	Courge f, patisson m
Marshmallow	Pâte de guimauve m
Marshmallow plant	Guimauve f
Marzipan	Massepain m

Matches	Allumettes f plural
Mayonnaise	Mayonnaise f
Mayonnaise, spicy garlic	Rouille f
Mead	Hydromel m
Meadow	Pré m
Meal	Repas m
Meat	Viande f
Meatball	Fricadelle f
Medium (as wine)	Demi-sec
Medium-cooked	Point, à
Megrim	Cardine f
Mellow	Moelleux, moelleuse
Melon	Melon m
Melted	Fondu
Melting	Fondant
Menu	Carte f
Menu, set	Table d'hôte f, prix fixe m
Meringue	Meringue f
Midday	Midi m
Milk	Lait m, lait entier m
Mill	Moulin m
Mince	Biftek haché m
Minced	Haché, hachée
Minced beef	Boeuf haché m
Minced meat	Hachis m
Mineral	Minéral, minérale
Mineral water	Minérale, eau f
Mint	Menthe f
Mint, wild	Pouliot m
Mixture	Mélange m
Monkfish	Lotte, baudroie f
Moray eel	Murène f

More	Plus, encore
More, some	Encore de
Morsel	Morceau m
Mother	Mère f
Mould	Galantine f, timbale f
Moulded	Moulé, moulée
Mountain	Montagne f
Mulberry	Mûre f
Mulled wine	Vin chaud
Mullet, grey	Mulet m
Mullet, grey	Muge f
Mullet, red	Rouget m
Multicoloured	À l'arlequin
Mushroom	Champignon m
Mussel	Moule f
Mussel stew	Mouclade f
Mussels, cooked in wine	Moules, à la marinière f
Mustard	Moutarde f
Muzzle	Museau m
Myrtle	Myrte m

Napkin	Serviette f
Nasturtium	Capucine f
Neck	Cou m
Neck label (wine)	Collerette f
Neck, of mutton	Collet m
Nectarine	Nectarine f
Needlefish	Balaou m
Nest	Nid m
Nettle	Ortie f
New	Nouveau, nouvelle
New wine	Primeur m
New Year's Eve	Saint-Sylvestre f
Next	Suivant
Noodles	Nouilles f
Noodles, small	Nouillettes f
North	Nord
Nose (as wine)	Bouquet m
Nougat	Nougat m
Nut	Noix f
Nutcracker	Casse-noix f
Nutmeg	Muscade m

Oatmeal	Gruau d'avoine m
Oats	Avoine f
Octopus	Poulpe m
Offal	Abats m
Oil	Huile f
Oil, groundnut	Huile d'arachides f
Oil, olive	Huile d'olive f
Oil, sunflower seed	Huile de tournesol f
Oil, virgin olive	Huile d'olive vierge f
Oil, walnut	Huile de noix f
Okra	Gombaut m
Old	Vieux, vieille
Olive	Olive f
Omelette	Omelette f
On	Sur
Onion	Oignon m
Onion rings, fried	Paillette d'oignon f
Onion stew	Oignonade f
Onion, spring	Ciboule f
Open	Ouvert, ouverte
Orange	Orange f
Orange, bitter	Bigarade f
Orange, blood	Sanguine f
Orange, mandarin	Mandarine f
Order	Commande f
Order, to	Commander
Ordinary	Ordinaire

Oregano	Origan m
Oven	Four m
Oven-roasted	Rôti au four
Over-ripe	Blet
Owner	Patron, propriétaire m/f
Ox-tripe	Gras-double m
Oxtail	Queue de boeuf f
Oyster	Huitre f
Oyster, cultivated	Huitre de parc f
Oyster, on the shell	Huitre en écaille f
Oystershell	Écaille d'huitre f

Pale	Blond, blonde
Palm hearts	Coeurs de palmier m
Pan	Poêle f
Pancake, thick	Pannequet m
Pancake, buckwheat	Tourtou m
Pancake, thin	Crêpe f
Papaya	Papaye f
Paper package	Papillotte f
Paprika	Paprika m
Parish	Commune f
Parsley	Persil m
Parsnip	Panais m
Parson's nose	Croupion m
Partridge	Perdrix f, perdreau m
Partridge, young	Perdreau m
Partridge, young	Pouillard m
Party (feast)	Fête f
Passion fruit	Barbadine f
Pasta	Pâtes alimentaires f
Paste	Pâté f
Paste, olive	Tapenade f
Paste, almond	Pâte d'amandes f
Pastry	Pâte f
Pastry case	Vol-au-vent m
Pastry shop	Pâtisserie f
Pastry strips	Allumettes f

Pastry, chou	Pâte à chou f
Pastry, sweet	Pâte sablée f
Paté	Pâté m
Paté, country-style	Pâté de campagne m
Paté, homemade	Pâté maison m
Paw	Patte f
Pay, to	Payer
Pea	Pois m
Pea, snow	Mange-tout m
Peach	Pêche f
Peach, yellow	Pêche abricotée f
Peach, white	Pêche blanche f
Peach, yellow	Pêche jaune f
Peanut	Cacahouète f, arachide f
Pear	Poire f
Pear spirit	Poire William f
Pearl	Perle f
Peas	Petit pois m
Peasant	Paysan, paysanne f
Peel	Écorce f
Pepper	Poivre m
Pepper, black	Poivre noir m
Pepper, sweet	Piment doux m
Pepper, sweet	Poivron m
Pepper, white	Poivre blanc m
Peppercorns	Poivre en grains m
Peppermill	Moulin à poivre m
Peppery	Poivré
Perch	Perche f, sandre m
Perch, sea	Serran m
Perch, young	Perchette f
Persimmon	Kaki m
Pheasant	Faisan m

Pheasant, young	Faisandeau m
Pickle, spicy fruit	Achard f
Pickled	Saumuré
Picnic	Pique-nique m
Pie	Pâté f
Pie, sweet	Tourte
Pie dish	Tourtière f
Pie, meat	Pâté f
Pig	Cochon m
Pig, suckling	Cochon de lait m
Pigeon	Pigeon m
Pigeon, wild	Palombe f
Pigeon, wood	Ramier m
Pigeon, young	Pigeonneau m
Pigeon, young wood	Ramereau m
Piglet	Cochonnet m
Pike	Brochet m
Pike, small	Brocheton m
Pilotfish	Poisson pilote m
Pine kernel	Pignon m
Pine tree	Pin m
Pineapple	Ananas m
Pink	Rosé, rosée
Pink peppercorn	Baies rosés
Piperfish	Grondin lyre m
Piquant	Piquant
Pistachio	Pistache f
Pitcher	Pichet m
Place	Lieu m
Placed	Mis en place
Plaice	Plie f
Plain	Simple
Plain (unadulterated)	Nature

Plate	Assiette f
Plate of hors d'oeuvres	Assiette assortie f
Plate, dish	Plat m
Platter, wooden	Planche f
Plover	Pluvier m
Pluck (offal)	Fressure f
Plum	Prune f
Plum, small yellow	Mirabelle f
Plum pudding	Pouding de Noël m
Plum tree	Prunier m
Poached	Poché, pochée
Pod	Cosse f, gousse f
Poison	Poison m
Pollack	Lieu jaune m
Pomegranate	Grenade f
Pomfret	Fiatole f
Poppy	Pavot m
Poppy, wild	Coquelicot m
Poppyseeds	Pavot, grains de m
Pork	Porc m
Pork fat	Lard m
Pork, potted	Graisserons m
Pork, salt	Petit salé m
Pork, spare ribs	Travers de porc m
Porridge, oatmeal	Porridge m, bouillie d'avoin f
Port	Porto m
Pot, earthenware	Casse f
Pot	Pot m
Pot, lidded	Poêlon m
Potato	Pomme de terre f
Potato, sweet	Patate f
Potato chips	Pommes frites f

Potato crisps	Chips m
Potato, baked	Pommes de terre, au four f
Potato, mashed	Purée de pommes f
Pot roasted	Poêlé, poêlée
Poultry	Volaille f
Poultry, offal	Béatilles f
Powder	Poudre f
Prawn	Crevette f
Prawn, large	Gamba f
Preserve	Conserve f
Preserved	Confit
Pressed	Pressé, pressée
Pressure	Pression f
Pretzel	Pretzel m
Price	Prix m
Prickly pear	Figue de barbarie f
Processed cheese	Fromage fondu f
Property	Propriété f
Proprietor	Patron, patronne, propriétaire
Prune	Pruneau m
Pudding, steamed	Pudding m
Pumpkin	Citrouille f, potiron m
Purée	Purée f
Purple	Poupre, violet

Quail	Caille f
Quail, young	Caillette f
Quarter	Quart m
Quince	Coing m
Quincepaste	Cotignac m

Rabbit	Lapin m
Rabbit, young	Lapereau m
Rack (of lamb)	Carré m
Radish	Radis m
Rainbow	Arc-en-ciel m
Raisin	Raisin sec m
Ramekin	Ramequin m
Rare	Saignant
Rare, very	Bleu
Raspberry	Framboise f
Ravioli	Raviolis m
Raw	Croque-au-sel, cru
Ready	Prêt
Recipe	Recette f
Recommended	Conseillé
Red	Rouge
Red mullet	Rouget m, rouget barbet m
Red pepper	Cayenne f
Red wine	Vin rouge
Redcurrant	Groseille f
Refined	Affiné
Reheated	Rechauffée
Rennet	Azi m
Reservation	Réservation f
Rhubarb	Rhubarbe f
Ribbon	Cordon m, ruban m

Ribboned	Rubané, rubanée
Rice	Riz m
Rice pudding	Riz au lait m
Rice, brown	Riz complet m
Rich	Riche
Rind (as lemon)	Écorce f
Rinds, pork	Couennes f
Ripe	Point, à
River	Rivière m
Roach	Gardon m
Roastbeef	Rosbif m
Roasted	Roti
Rock	Rocher m
Rock cake	Casse-museau m, rocher m
Rock salmon	Roussette f
Rockling	Motelle f
Rocksalt, seasalt	Gros sel m
Roe	Laitance f
Roe, dried	Poutarge f
Rolled	Roulé, roulée
Rollmop	Hareng roulé m
Root	Racine f
Rose wine	Vin rosé m
Rosehip	Gratte-cul f
Rosemary	Romarin m
Rot	Pourriture f
Rotten	Pourri
Rough	Rude
Rowan	Sorbe f
Rum	Rhum m
Rump, of beef	Pièce f, culotte de boeuf f
Runny	Baveur, baveuse
Rusk	Biscotte f

Russet	Roux, rousse
Russet apple	Reinette grise f
Rye	Seigle m

Saddle, as lamb	Selle f
Saddle, as rabbit	Râble m
Saffron	Safran m
Sage	Sauge f
Sago	Sagou m
Sailor	Marin m
Salad	Salade f
Salad bowl	Saladier m
Salad dressing	Vinaigrette f
Salad, green	Salade verte f
Salad, mixed	Salade composée f, salade panachée f
Salami	Saucisson sec m, salamis m
Salmon	Saumon m
Salmon, rock	Saumonette f
Salmon, smoked	Saumon fumé m
Salmon, young	Saumoneau m
Salmon-trout	Truite de mer f
Salsify	Salsifis m
Salt	Sel m
Salt, sea	Sel marin m
Salt cod	Morue f
Salt marsh	Pré-salé m
Salt pork	Salé, petit m
Salt, coarse rock	Sel gris m
Salt, table	Sel de table m
Salted	Salé, salée

Salted, lightly	Demi-sel
Salted herring	Hareng salé m, hareng saur m
Saltfree	Sans sel
Samphire	Fenouil marin m, christ-marin m
Sand	Sable m
Sand sole	Sole polé f
Sand-dab	Fausse-sole f
Sand-eel	Équille f, lançon m
Sandpiper	Alouette de mer f
Sandsmelt	Melet m
Sandwich	Sandwich m
Sardine	Sardine f
Sardines, tinned	Sardines à l'huile f
Sardines, very tiny	Poutine f
Sauce	Sauce f
Saucepan	Casserole f
Saucer	Soucoupe f
Saury	Balaou m
Sausagemeat	Chair à saucisse f
Sausage spread	Tartinette f
Sausage, fresh, uncooked	Saucisse f
Sausage, thin spicy	Merguez f
Sausage, tripe	Andouillette f
Savory	Sarriette f
Scabbard fish	Sabre m
Scad	Chinchard m
Scalded	Échaudé
Scaled	Écaillé
Scallop	Coquille St Jacques f
Scallop, small queen	Pétoncle m
Scampi	Grosse crevette f, langoustine f

Scorpion fish	Rascasse f
Scrambled	Brouillé, brouillée
Scrambled eggs	Oeufs brouillés m
Sea	Mer f
Sea kale	Chou marin m
Sea-anemone	Anémone de mer f
Sea-lamprey	Lamproie marine m
Sea-slug	Bêche de mer f
Sea-turtle	Tortue de mer f
Sea-urchin	Oursin m
Seabass	Loup de mer m, bar m
Seafood	Fruits de mer m
Season	Saison f
Seasonal	Saissonier
Seasoned	Assaisonné
Seasoning	Assaisonnement m
Seat	Siège m
Seaweed	Algues f
Seed	Graine f
Segment	Quartier m
Semi-skimmed milk	Lait demi-écremé m
Semi-sparkling	Moustille
Semolina	Semoule f
Served	Servi, servie
Service	Service m
Service charge	Service m
Service included	Service compris
Service not included	Service non compris
Setting	Couvert m
Shad	Alose f
Shallot	Échalote f
Shandy	Panaché m
Share, to	Partager

Shark	Requin m
Shark, hammerhead	Requin marteau m
Sheep	Mouton m
Shell	Coque f
Shellfish	Coquillage f
Shepherd's pie	Hachis parmentier m
Sherry	Xérès m
Shin	Jarret m
Shoulder	Épaule f
Shrimp	Crevette f
Shrimp, brown	Crevette grise f
Simmer, to (liquid)	Frémir
Simmer, to (stew)	Mijoter
Sirloin	Aloyau m
Size	Grandeur m, grosseur m
Size, according to	Selon grosseur (s.g.)
Skate	Raie f
Skate, small	Raiteau m, raiton m
Skewer	Brochette f
Skimmed milk	Lait écremé m
Skin	Peau, peaux f
Skinned, shelled	Derobé
Slice, round	Rouelle, rondelle, f
Slice, thick	Tranche f, darne f
Slice, very thin	Lèche f
Sliced bread	Mie, pain de m
Slimness	Minceur m
Slip sole	Solette f
Sloe	Prunelle f
Slopes	Coteaux m
Small	Petit, petite
Smell	Odeur, f, parfum m
Smelly	Puant, puante

Smelt	Éperlan m
Smoke, to	Fumer
Smoked	Fumé, fumée
Smoked haddock	Haddock m
Snack	Snack m, lèger repas m
Snail	Escargot m
Snail, small	Cagouille f, aspergille f
Snipe	Bécassine f
Snipe, young	Bécau m
Snow	Neige f
Soda water	Eau de seltz f
Soft	Mou, mol, molle
Soft-boiled eggs	Oeufs mollets m
Softish	Mollet, mollette
Sole	Sole f
Sole, speckled	Sole f, tachetée f
Sorrel	Oseille f
Sorrel, wild	Surelle f
Soup	Soupe f
Soup, clear	Consommé m
Soup, thickened	Potage m
Sour	Aigre
Sourcream	Crème fraîche f
South	Sud
Soya bean	Graine de soja f
Soya bean oil	Huile de soja f
Sparkling (wine)	Pétillant, mousseux
Sparkling wine	Vin mousseux
Sparkling, slightly	Perlant, perlé
Speciality	Spécialité f
Spice	Épice f
Spicy	Pimentée
Spinach	Épinards m

Spirit, clear	Alcool-blanc m
Spit-roasted	Broche, à la
Spleen	Rate f
Splitpeas	Pois casseś m
Spoon	Cuillère f
Sprat	Esprot m, haringuet m
Spring	Source f
Spring, the season	Printemps m
Square	Carré
Squash, vegetable	Patisson m
Squid	Calmar m
Stag	Cerf m
Stale, as bread	Rassis, rassise
Star	Étoile f
Starch	Fécule f
Starter	Hors d'oeuvre f
Steak	Steack m, biftek, m
Steak, chopped	Steack haché m
Steak, medium	Steack à point m
Steak, raw (tartare)	Steack tartare m
Steak, rib	Entrecôte f
Steak, round fillet	Tournedos m
Steak, saignant	Steack saignant m
Steak, rare	Steack bleu m
Steak, well-done	Steack bien cuit m
Steam	Vapeur f
Stew, of meat, game or poultry	Ragout m, civet m
Stew, of freshwater fish	Matelote f
Stew, of pork, goose and beans	Cassoulet m
Stewed	Étuvé
Stewed fruit	Compote f

Stewpot	Daubière f, marmite f
Stock	Fumet m, bouillon m
Stock-cube	Bouillon-cube m
Stomach	Estomac m
Strained	Passé, passée
Straw	Paille f
Strawberry	Fraise f
Strawberry, wild	Fraise des bois f
Strips, thin	Julienne f
Strong	Fort, forte
Stuffed	Farci, fourré, étouffé
Stuffing	Farce f
Stuffing, veal	Godiveau m
Sturgeon	Esturgeon m
Style	Manière, à la
Style, in the	Mode, à la
Suckling pig	Cochon de lait m, porcelet n
Suet	Graisse de rognon f
Sugar	Sucre m
Sugar, brown	Sucre brun m, sucre roux m
Sugar, cane	Sucre de canne m
Sugar, caster	Sucre en poudre m
Sugar, cubes	Sucre en morceaux m
Sugar, granulated	Sucre cristallisé m
Sugar, icing	Sucre glace m
Suggest, to	Proposer
Summer	Été m
Sunflower	Tournesol m
Sunflower seed oil	Huile de tournesol f
Supper	Souper
Surprise	Surprise f
Swallow	Hirondelle f
Swan	Cygne m

Swede	Rutabaga m, chou-navet m
Sweet	Doux, douce
Sweet	Bonbon m
Sweet and sour	Aigre-doux
Sweet, small	Pastille f
Sweetbreads	Ris m
Sweetened	Sucré, sucrée
Sweetmeat	Gourmandise f, friandise f
Swiss	Suisse
Sword	Sabre m
Swordfish	Espadon m
Syrup	Sirop m

Table	Table f
Table wine	Vin de table m
Tail	Queue f
Take-away, to	Emporter
Tap	Robinet m
Tapioca	Perle du Japon f, tapioca m
Tap water	Eau de robinet f
Tarragon	Estragon m
Tart	Tarte f
Tart, apple	Tarte tatin f
Tart, savoury egg	Quiche f
Tart, small	Tartelette f
Taste	Goût m
Tasteless	Insipide
Taste, to	Goûter
Tasting	Dégustation f
Tea with lemon	Thé m
Tea with milk	Tilleul, infusion de m
Tea, herbal	Tisane f
Tea, with lemon	Thé au citron m
Tea, with milk	Thé au lait m
Tea-caddy	Boîte à thé f
Teal	Avocet m
Teapot	Théière f
Tearoom	Salon de thé m
Teaspoon	Cuillère à thé f, à café f

Tempting	Péche
Tench	Tanche f
Tenderised	Attendri
Testicles, lamb	Animelles f
Thickening (for sauce)	Liaison f
Thigh	Cuisse f
Thrush	Grive f
Thyme	Thym m
Thyme, wild	Serpolet m, farigoule f
Tin (can)	Boîte f
Tin (metal)	Étain
Tin-opener	Ouvre-boîte f
Tinfoil	Papier d'aluminium m
Tip	Gratuité f, pourboires m
Tip (end)	Pointe f
Tipple, to	Picoler
Toast, thin, dry	Melba toast
Today	Aujourd'hui
Tomato	Tomate f
Tomato sauce	Ketchup aux tomates, sauce tomate
Tomorrow	Demain
Tongue	Langue f
Tongue, ox	Langue de boeuf
Tonight	Ce soir
Toothpick	Cure-dent m
Topside, veal	Gite m, fricandeau m
Tossed	Sauté, sautée
Traditional	Ancienne, à l'
Tray	Plateau m
Treacle	Mélasse f
Triggerfish	Baliste f

Tripe	Bétise f
Tripe	Tripes f, betises f
Trolley	Chariot m
Trotter, pigs'	Pied de porc m
Trout	Truite f
Trout, brown	Truite rivière f
Trout, rainbow	Truite, arc-en-ciel f
Trout, salmon	Truite saumonée
Truffle	Truffe f
Tuna	Thon m
Tuna, small	Thonine f
Turbot	Turbot m
Turbot, small	Turbotin m
Turkey, cock	Dindon m
Turkey, hen	Dinde f
Turkey, young	Dindonneau m
Turmeric	Curcuma f, safran des Indes m
Turnip	Navet m
Turtle	Tortue f

Udder	Tétine f
Ugli fruit	Aegle m
Uncork, to	Déboucher
Under	Sous
Undrinkable	Imbuvable, non potable
Unleavened	Azyme
Unrefined	Brut
Unsweetened	Brut

V.A.T.	T.V.A.
Vacuum-packed	Sous vide
Vanilla	Vanille f
Varied	Divers
Vat	Cuve f
Veal	Veau m
Vegetable	Légume m
Vegetables, raw	Crudités f
Vegetables, green	Verdure f
Vegetarian	Végétarien, végétarienne
Venison	Venaison f, chevreuil m
Verbena	Verveine f
Vermicelli	Vermicelle m
Vermouth	Vermouth m
Vine	Vigne f
Vine twigs	Sarments m
Vinegar	Vinaigre m
Vineyard	Vignoble m
Vineyard, enclosed	Clos m
Vintage	Millesime m, année f
Violet	Violette f
Virgin, as oil	Vierge f

Waffle	Gaufre f
Waiter, waitress	Serveur m, serveuse f
Walnut	Noix f
Walnut, green	Cerneau m
Warm	Tiède
Warm, to (especially a wine)	Chambrer
Washing-up	Vaiselle f
Water	Eau f
Watermelon	Pastèque f
Water, drinking	Eau potable f
Water, fresh	Eau douce f
Water, sparkling mineral	Eau minérale avec gaz f
Water, still mineral	Eau minérale sans gaz f
Water, tap	Eau de robinet f
Water, undrinkable	Eau non potable f
Waterchestnut	Châtaigne d'eau f, macre m
Watercress	Cresson m
Weever	Vive f
Well-done	Bien cuit
West	Ouest
Wet one's whistle, to	Réboucher
Wheat	Blé m, froment m
Wheatgerm	Germe de blé, f
Whelk	Buccin m
Whey	Petit lait m

Whipped	Fouettée
Whisky	Whisky m
White	Blanc, blanche
White pudding	Boudin blanc m
White wine	Vin blanc
Whitebait	Blanchailles f
Whiting	Merlan m
Whole	Entier, entière
Whole, as bread	Complet
Wholemeal	Bis
Wild	Sauvage
Wild boar	Sanglier m, marcassin m
Wild duck	Canard sauvage m
Wine lover	Amateur de vin m
Wing, of poultry	Aile f
Winkle	Bignorneau m
Winter	Hiver m
Wishbone	Bréchet m, fourchette f
With	Avec
Wood	Bois m
Woodcock	Bécasse f
Woodcock, young	Bécasseau m
Wrapping	Fichu
Wrasse	Crenilabre m, labre m

Yam	Igname f
Yeast	Levure f
Yellow	Jaune
Yoghurt	Yaourt m, yoghurt m

Zest	Zeste m

Recommended Reading and Bibliography

New Larousse Gastronomique, Prosper Montagne, BCA
A–Z Gastronomique: Sharman and Chadwick, Papermac
Pocket Guide to French Food and Wine: Youell and Kimball, Xanadu
French Food and France: Richard Binns, Waymark
ABC of French Food: Len Deighton, Century Hutchinson
International Foodbook: Quentin Crewe, Hatchards
Mediterranean Seafood: Alan Davidson, Penguin
Food: Waverley Root, Simon and Schuster
The Taste of France: Freson, Hamlyn
Escoffier: Cracknell and Kaufmann, Heinemann
La Cuisine Provencale: J–B. Reboul, Tecussel
La Cuisine Bretonne D'Aujourd'hui; Le Roy, Solar
La Repertoire de la Cuisine: Gringoire et Saulnier, Flammarion
Moi, Le Fromage et Vous: Hubert, Dargaud
Le Nouveau Livre de Cuisine: Caramel, Gautier-Languereau
La Bonne Cuisine de la Mer: Piccinardi, Solar
Poissons, Coquillages et Crustaces: Colinet, Grund
Wine, A Consumer's Guide: Anthony Lamont, Collins Gem
Guide to French Wines: Steven Spurrier, Salem House
World Wine Encyclopaedia: Tom Stevenson, Dorling Kindersley

Encyclopaedia of Wines and Spirits: Alexis Lichine, Cassell
French Red and Rosé Wine: Oz Clarke, Websters
French White Wines: Oz Clarke, Websters
Lexivin, Paul Cadiau, Paul Cadiau Publr